For Bill Tolley, a
University President who
still makes time to read.

DIPLOMACY IN A DEMOCRACY

☆

☆

☆

☆

DIPLOMACY

☆

☆

☆

☆

IN A DEMOCRACY

by Henry M. Wriston

HARPER & BROTHERS, NEW YORK

TO

M. W. W.

CONTENTS

PREFACE

This volume is based upon lectures given at the Associated Colleges at Claremont, California, which include Claremont College, Claremont Men's College, Pomona College, and Scripps College. They are the fifteenth series in a lectureship established in 1940 and sponsored by some one hundred friends of these institutions.

I was asked at the time to expand the lectures somewhat beyond the limits which are available to a lecturer. The substance remains unchanged, though there is some expansion of the discussion and illustration.

I want to express my gratitude to Dr. Robert J. Bernard, the Managing Director, and to the Presidents of the colleges, George C. S. Benson, E. Wilson Lyon, and Frederick Hard. All made the occasion of the lectures an interesting and rewarding experience and have been most generous in their thoughtful comment.

I am again deeply indebted to Miss Ruth E. Sandborn, who, in this instance as on many previous occasions, has been of invaluable help as research associate, editor, and critic. I owe an especial debt of gratitude also to Mrs. Dorothea T. Borden, whose patience, intelligence, and secretarial skill survived making many drafts.

I wish to express my thanks to Little, Brown and Company for permission to quote, in several places, from two volumes by Walter Lippmann, *Essays in the Public Philosophy* and *U.S. Foreign Policy: Shield of the Republic.*

book I

DEMOCRACY

AND THE PROFESSIONAL DIPLOMAT

1

The Setting

The Foreign Service Officer corps has been virtually invisible throughout the larger part of its half century or more of history. This is not peculiar or abnormal. Most of the officers are stationed abroad; they are out of the public eye except upon relatively rare occasions. They may draw some attention in the countries to which they are accredited by their tact or lack of it, by their social activities, by their public appearances on specific occasions. But their effectiveness is in almost inverse ratio to their conspicuousness. It is not only bad form, it is bad diplomacy, for them to win "victories." Such "triumphs" are hollow, for they are bound to

3

injure domestically the government with which the diplomat has to deal, and make future relationships and negotiations more difficult, needlessly.

When Foreign Service officers are at home they are apt to be even more inconspicuous. They wear no uniforms, and if they have decorations the evidences of such honors do not appear in public. If they bear a title it is likely to be a relatively unfamiliar one in the Department of State; there any achievement becomes, by long tradition, that of the Secretary. He is the man who receives both the applause for "success" and the blame for "failure" in our foreign policy.

In recent years there have been a number of occasions when the visibility of our Foreign Service has been uncharacteristically high. As is the case with much of the news, these instances have usually been associated with trouble. The collapse of Nationalist China's power on the mainland and the swift rise to virtually complete control by Mao Tze-tung and his Communist cohorts were dramatic. This change was a severe setback to American policy. Our heavy commitments to the Nationalist cause were symbolized by President Roosevelt's insistence, over the objections of Winston Churchill, that China be treated as a great power and given one of the permanent seats on the Security Council of the United Nations.

Even before the dramatic collapse of our China policy, a more generalized factor became evident. After years of coexistence with communism and a period of informal alliance during the war, its inherently aggressive nature was brought home to millions of Americans by its rape of Poland, the destruction and absorption of the Baltic states, its reduction to satellitism of most of Eastern Europe, and the menace of an advance into Western Europe. Under these circumstances the Communist sweep in China and the aggression in Korea were bound to bring acute public unease.

When any national policy suffers a conspicuous setback, there is certain to be a hunt for scapegoats upon whom the blame for the disaster can be loaded. That is as inevitable as anything political can be, and it is equally true in a totalitarian or a democratic regime. The manner in which Khrushchev and Bulganin made the dead Beria the scapegoat for the failure of Stalin's policy regarding Jugoslavia is a familiar instance in point. In the United States a natural target in any search for causes of disaster was the Department of State and the Foreign Service.

The opposition party was certain to attribute our "failures" in policy to indifference or incompetence upon the part of those responsible for it; and probes were equally certain to penetrate through the top layer of political officials into the lower layers of professional diplomats. The Hiss case, the allegations regarding Harry Dexter White became symbolic. The fact that neither was part of the Foreign Service was bound to be overlooked, for the differentiation between the Civil Service and the Foreign Service is not generally understood, much less appreciated. The defection of Guy Burgess and Donald Maclean, both British Foreign Service officers holding responsible positions, raised questions as to the infiltration of our own Service.

When these events were combined with the first change in twenty years in the political complexion of the executive branch of the Federal government, a spate of Congressional investigations was inevitable. At the same time, by executive order, the President established new and much more rigid security requirements and all officers had to be "cleared" once again. This was not only to weed out subversives and weaklings; it was to give the public full assurance of the integrity of the government service as a whole.

Thus the Foreign Service came to public attention under the most unfavorable auspices. Some politicians asserted that it had been less than astute; a few maintained that it had been infiltrated with Communists, and even spies. The Yalta Conference was reviewed and the parts played by individuals discussed, often with more venom than perception. A few members of the Foreign Service were dismissed, permitted to resign, or retired. Usually each instance was accompanied by wide publicity; and the consideration of the cases was so deliberate in pace as to prolong public discussion needlessly. Moreover, some investigations were challenged as to their character, thoroughness, impartiality, and respect for Constitutional principles.

This unwelcome spotlight produced a change in atmosphere. At the same time an economy drive involved a reduction in force. Furthermore, a number of Foreign Service officers were retired before their normal expectation by the application of new and more drastic performance standards which had nothing to do with security, yet became associated with that issue in the public mind because the actions on the two separate bases were contemporaneous.

A number of diplomats who come under none of these categories believed that the reputation of the Service had been needlessly smirched, and that the Secretary of State did not show adequate appreciation of the Service, or give it the firm support its past performances merited. There was a strong feeling that irrelevant political considerations were affecting adversely the established professional character of the Service. Moreover, there were new regulations, that seemed unfair, regarding leaves and other rights recognized by law. In consequence, a number of admirable officers resigned, and the heavy investment of the government in their training and experience was lost.

The diplomat best known to the public, after retirement from the Service, asserted that even before the new administration took office the Foreign Service "was weakened beyond real hope of recovery," was an "administrative ruin," "demoralized by anonymous security agents, . . . a helpless object of disparagement and defamation at the hands of outside critics." He concluded that "the experiment of professional diplomacy, as undertaken by the United States in 1925, had failed." Portions of the press joined in these gloomy conclusions and asserted that the morale of the Service had been "shattered."

The accuracy of such statements could be neither precisely demonstrated nor statistically refuted. But some hard facts were clear. The Foreign Service had, indeed, stopped growing. All recruitment had been suspended during the war and the deficiencies caused by that action had not been repaired by vigorous recruitment when the war was over. Moreover, for reasons difficult to conceive, no new appointments to the Service were made in the later months of the Truman administration. Even before this inexplicable failure to act, the procedures for examination and appointment had become so clumsy and inept that it took from two to three years for the applicant to pass all his examinations, be accepted as an officer, and receive an assignment. In a period of saturated employment this meant that many, or most, of the eligibles had taken other positions before the bureaucratic machinery had finally functioned. It is not surprising, therefore, that the number of young men and women applying for examination shrank alarmingly.

No one long acquainted with the problem or sensitive to current realities could assert that the situation was a healthy

one. It was natural, indeed inevitable, that under such circumstances there should be a renewal of a question, debated
many times before, whether the United States, as a democracy, could or would support a really professional foreign
service. A vigorous critic quoted with apparent acceptance
an aphorism of Jules Cambon, a long-time French foreign
officer of an earlier day. He had asserted that "while democracies would always have diplomacy, it was a question
whether they would ever have diplomatists." This negative
evaluation of the capacity of a democracy to have a truly
professional foreign service has had some rather impressive
endorsement, particularly as applied to the United States.

Certainly it would be difficult to make a strong case in
opposition if one looked at the matter only in short historical
perspective. Nonetheless there were some concrete facts
which did not appear in most of the public discussions. Despite all these vicissitudes, the number of dismissals, retire-
ments, and resignations was small relative to the whole
number of Foreign Service officers. Moreover, there remained
an able, experienced, and well-tested Service, whose members accepted with philosophic calm the special hazards of
their profession and stayed at their chosen task with faithful
efficiency. Since these people continued to be invisible and
almost anonymous, they were too easily forgotten in the excitement over the small minority whose public prominence
was so great.

In any event, our judgment regarding the capacity of a
democracy to use the talents of professional diplomats should
be based upon the fact that history is long. It is a fatal mistake to judge trends upon a short base line. There are bound
to be periods of storm and stress; this generation has lived in
such an era. Two world wars in one lifetime are sufficient to
distort any but long range perspective. More particularly it

is easy to feel that democracy itself is on the wane, that it reached an apogee at the moment of victory in 1918 and has since been in decline—some would call it precipitous decline.

That its expansion has virtually halted is true, at least for the moment, but some of its earlier "advances" were in reality illusory. Several nations were not adapted to the growth of democracy; some seeds "fell by the wayside, . . . some fell upon stony places, where they had not much earth . . . and some fell among thorns." Perhaps we should study our soil chemistry more attentively, prepare the ground better, and sow with a less lavish or wasteful hand. No nation with a mature democracy or indigenous democratic institutions has abandoned them. Nor should we despair that some of the backsliding converts will again see the light and return to the democratic ideal as Italy and Germany seem in process of doing. Surely it will not help others to do so if America loses heart and betrays its birthright.

Under these circumstances, the reverses, transient as I believe most of them to be, do not justify Cambon's gloomy conclusion. It is too large a generalization based upon too short an experience in an adverse atmosphere.

I propose to express a reasoned view in opposition to current pessimism on that point. My thesis is that a sound professional diplomatic corps is neither impeded, on the one hand, nor guaranteed, on the other, by the fact of democracy. Bringing in the question of democracy and making that type of government the decisive factor, if not entirely irrelevant, at least severely distort correct perspective. The existence of a permanent body of expert diplomatists is determined basically by two factors: the position of a nation in world affairs and public appreciation of the significance of that position. General awareness of grave peril makes the public suspicious of amateurs, many of whom are so politically motivated as to jeopardize the national interest and endanger peace by partisan strife. Acute danger stimulates a demand for experienced and competent diplomatists.

That we live in an era of deadly peril is unquestioned. The fundamental postulates of the two dominant political, social, and economic systems are so deeply at variance, and the consequent tensions between them are so critical, that it remains to be seen whether collision and armed conflict can be avoided. Reduced to its simplest terms, that is the question the world now faces. The issue of peace or war is vital not only to Russia and its satellites and to the United States and its allies; it is just as instant a problem to all men everywhere. The power of thermonuclear weapons is so great and growing so fast, and the means for their delivery are multiplying in numbers and effectiveness so rapidly, that the survival of mankind seems to many to hang in the balance of the decision. In this instance terror arises not from the nameless fears of the ignorant or superstitious; it flows from the calculations of the best informed. The urgency of the matter is most real to those who know most about it.

Since the powers of the principal protagonists are so nearly in balance, the answer to the question of peace or war must rest with diplomacy, which thus becomes decisively important. It is the only channel of communication open to all the interested parties. The problem of communication might be less difficult if there were just two entities, the Soviets and their satellites on the one hand and the United States with its allies on the other. Outside these two aggregates, however, are many nations with varying degrees of affinity for one group or the other, or doggedly insistent upon neutrality.

Ten years ago, in 1946, the concept of a bipolar world had a certain plausibility; even that has now disappeared. At that time the power of Germany and Japan had been destroyed not only militarily but also economically and politically. India, Burma, Ceylon were still British; Indonesia was Dutch; Indochina was French. The Arab world was not yet aflame with nationalism; the British held Suez; the French grip upon North Africa was unshaken. Since the end of the second World War over 600 million people have been released from colonial status and ushered into independence. That represents the largest group of events of its kind in world history. Vast Afro-Asian populations are keenly aware of and acutely jealous of their new status. West Germany has shown a high order of economic and political recovery and Japan is returning, more slowly, to a strong position in the international world.

These changes are reflected in the United Nations among other places. It would overstate the case to assert that a "third force" has come into being; the interests, ambitions, and methods of the new and renewed nations are too diverse to justify any such generalization. The Bandung Conference, nevertheless, gave reason to believe such a force may develop, and the spokesmen of India occasionally seem to suggest it has already done so.

In such circumstances, any thought of bipolarity has become an anachronism. The effort to draw all the neutralists into our diplomatic orbit runs counter to our own earlier passion for independence from external influence and resistance to the continuation of our French alliance made during the Revolution. New and weak states are supersensitive. Pressure upon them to conform to our ideas is more likely to produce a violent reaction away from us than to induce adherence. There is already clear evidence of that truth. The disappearance of the possibility of bipolarity has not simplified diplomacy; on the contrary it has brought to the surface tensions and difficulties which had heretofore been latent and submerged. Now they are released, one might almost say rampant. This lays upon the diplomat new tasks of almost unique subtlety and complexity.

Further evidence that the bipolar concept was never actually valid lies in the fact that neither the Soviet bloc nor the Western alliance is solid. We are apt to attribute a monolithic quality to the Soviet group. To do so is to shut our eyes to important truths; within that entity there are strains, some of them serious. Russian and Chinese policies, for example, are not now uniform in all respects and the differences between them may widen with the passage of time. Communist ideology in the two nations is far from consistent, and national interests may come to transcend the points of similarity and the need for each other which now hold them so closely together.

Divergencies in the Far Eastern policies of the United States and Britain hinge upon their varying estimates of this situation. Here occur the chief differences in the world-views of the two principal Western allies. British policy is predicated upon the assumption that the outlook of Russia and that of China reveal differences that may be exploited in order to reduce the intransigence of both nations. They can point to certain historical facts, such as the declaration of Mao twenty years ago that he intended to include Outer Mongolia in China. American policy, on the other hand, has tended to assume that China has only a satellite status in the Russian orbit. Evidences of error in this estimate have been concealed by domestic political passions. Such pressures have impaired flexibility of policy, and more particularly have prevented any exploitation of Sino-Soviet divergencies.

Even in Eastern Europe evidences of tension with some of the satellites appear from time to time. The break with

Jugoslavia provides a pertinent illustration. The violence
of the Stalin regime at manifestations of independence upon
the part of Tito was vicious in its intensity. Efforts to over-
throw the recalcitrant took many and extreme forms. Their
failure was conspicuous. The recent strenuous endeavors of
Khrushchev and Bulganin to heal the breach accentuated its
gravity. In order to recover lost ground the new Soviet
leaders set a precedent of the first order of importance for
Western diplomacy. They virtually endorsed the heresy of
national communism, which involves freedom from control
of the central party apparatus in Moscow. This change of
basic position was elaborated and endorsed by the twentieth
Congress of the Soviet Communist Party. Thus the way is
open for Western exploitation of this astonishing alteration
of policy through attempts to get other satellites to manifest
like deviationism, and break the power of their "little
Stalins," puppets of Moscow.

Western diplomats should now realize that Russian policy
must often take account of minority views. Shifts in its over-
all position are not infrequently a recognition in action of
this fact—a circumstance too little noticed in the United
States. Nevertheless, the mastery of Russia over its group
of satellites comes far closer to dominance than does the
leadership of the United States within its alliance.

So far as the Western alliance is concerned, there is no
chance that it could be made monolithic. The hazard is the
reverse. Centrifugal forces are always powerful within any
voluntary alliance of this sort, particularly in peace time.
Historically alliances have been held together much more
frequently and more firmly by external pressure; their in-
ternal cohesiveness has shown its weakness whenever the
outside force was slackened or removed. We have witnessed
this; Churchill summed it up when he remarked that when

Russia and the West lost their sole bond by the defeat of their common foe, the result was the destruction of the wartime alliance, and the implacable enmity of the Soviets toward the Western democracies. Alliances almost always are more effective in war than during peace. In war the external threat is instant and manifest; peace, even a "cold peace," makes danger seem more remote, and brings the divergent—indeed the conflicting—interests of the several allies to the fore.

In consequence it requires much more skill to preserve a peaceful defensive combination of nations than a wartime alliance. That is the reason so many people are alarmed when they see Molotov smile, and hear Khrushchev and Bulganin carry honeyed words to India, Burma, and Afghanistan. The cohesiveness of the Western alliance was helped again and again during the Stalinist era by Russian intransigence, bad manners, stupidity, and aggressiveness. Successive Soviet "peace offensives" were usually destroyed by their own ineptitude. The cordiality that followed the Summit Conference in Geneva in 1955, the joint talks about peace, a cooperative temper on minor issues—these put strains upon the Atlantic coalition that only the most skillful diplomacy could counter. The present state of affairs in Jugoslavia, Greece, and Turkey furnish a whole series of illustrations.

Some of the difficulties diplomacy has not mastered. Tito is now playing both ends to his own benefit; his ties with Greece and Turkey are correspondingly weakened; his relationships with Egypt have become more intimate. The demand in Cyprus for "enosis" with Greece has created grave difficulties with Turkey. The solidity of the "northern tier" has been weakened by peaceful gestures on the part of the Soviets and their exploitation of the difficulties Britain has in Cyprus between the Greek majority and the Turkish minority.

No one who understands the temper of the world or the interests of the United States would fail to do everything reasonable to relieve tension with the Soviets. But he would be blind not to see that every success in easing that pressure creates new problems in keeping the Atlantic alliance strong. The task of the diplomat is simultaneously to hold friends together and keep the potential enemy at bay. His left hand works against his right. If he does not reduce tensions he is hostile to peace; if he relieves strain the strength of the alliance is correspondingly endangered. The path of diplomacy in these circumstances is narrow indeed; nonetheless it has become of critical importance. The diplomat must expound and explain; he must report and interpret; he must negotiate. Whatever is necessary to keep the peace and protect the national interest must be channeled through him. No longer is his significance largely ceremonial, or his labors peripheral. He can make or break the peace.

2

The Diplomat

What kind of man should the diplomat be, and what relationship should he bear to the public and to elected officers? He must comprehend and remain sensitive to American public sentiment; that is fundamental. No matter how long his assignments keep him abroad he must never become alien to the temper which informs and directs public opinion at home. As though that were not task enough, he must be almost equally able to sense the temper and will of our allies. He must be as familiar with the political currents that flow through them as he is with those of the United States—and must maintain an attitude of detachment from both. He

16

must also be completely familiar with the potential enemy, able to read his thoughts and explain his actions. In this, also, he must be objective; passionate attachments and bitter antipathies each warp the cool judgment needed in diplomacy. It is no profession for the individual who is by nature a strong partisan. He must be understanding and sympathetic with the uncommitted peoples, even as he tries to gain their adherence to our system of alliances—or, at least, attempts to keep them out of the Soviet orbit.

His first qualification, therefore, is knowledge in both depth and breadth. Great stress must be laid on depth, which can best be defined as historical perspective. The age in which we live has novel and unique characteristics; no one should underestimate its differences from other times. But if it has unique qualities, it also shares many of its most vital characteristics with previous eras.

Speaking at the Council on Foreign Relations in New York on September 28, 1955, Harold Macmillan, then British Foreign Secretary, said: "The civilised world, at least the Western world, still draws its inspiration from two sources, the classical and the Biblical. . . . It is not clear that there is anything particular of much value, except on the scientific and technical side, which is being thought or said today which was not contained either in classical or Biblical literature two thousand years or more ago." While one need not accept that dictum too literally, it is a useful reminder that, though human nature changes, it alters but slowly, and the basic human reactions today are much like those of earlier ages. The more a diplomat is versed in history, the more fully he has entered imaginatively into crises ancient and modern, the better he will be equipped to deal with current crises.

This is particularly true of Russia. Many of the aggressive traits which now so occupy our minds long antedate the

Bolshevik revolution. Cyrus L. Sulzberger, foreign affairs columnist of the *New York Times,* published on February 4, 1956, a dispatch from an American envoy which, with the change of a few words, could be accepted as a description of the current situation, yet it was written more than a hundred years ago. "A strange superstition prevails among the Russians that they are destined to conquer the world. . . . Expediency is the great test. And what may be expedient today . . . may be inexpedient tomorrow." "Ministers are constantly subjected to a system of espionage." "One of the most disagreeable features . . . is the secrecy with which everything is done." "Nothing is attainable but after the most provoking delays. . . . I may mention that the late message of the President of the United States was not regarded in all its parts as a safe document for Russian readers and came to their hands scathed with the censor's knife." Russia's "vast military power and military spirit are the secrets" of its ascendancy over the rest of Europe, "aided by a system of diplomacy which has perhaps no equal." This is a fresh illustration of the applicability of the French aphorism, "The more things change, the more they remain the same." Historical perspective highlights the changes and the similarities with equal clarity.

Philosophy is inseparably linked to history. As a diplomat steeps himself in past experience and in the values which men have held most precious, he is preparing for his contemporary task. The more he ponders the varying reactions of persons whose philosophical presuppositions are different from his own, the better will he grasp their point of view. This is most obvious in dealing with Orientals; it requires profound knowledge of their philosophical background to perceive the deeper meaning of the all-too-obvious slogan, "Asia for the Asiatics." The French, the Germans, the Russians—indeed all peoples—have values bred into them through generations. The learned diplomat will know from earlier experiences that he has shared vicariously in his reading which assumptions are inflexible and must be circumvented, and which are plastic and can be adapted to new forms.

The modern diplomat cannot escape economics; but the more he knows of its discipline, the more surely he will be skeptical of simple economic explanations. Often I regret the passing of the old name, Political Economy. That designation is more pertinent now than it was when it had its widest currency. Trade, exchange rates and methods, tariffs, quotas, preferences, debts, loans—these are economic, indeed, but they are equally political. No one can say where the balance between the two sets of concepts rests at any given moment. Narrowly proficient economists who lack political insight claim that nearly every question has an economic basis. Their assertions are dangerously tainted with economic determinism which should be regarded as the sole property of the Soviets. Let the Communists have full possession of dialectic materialism with all the limitations such a philosophy puts upon breadth of view. But even when due regard is given to the interrelationship of problems, those which are primarily economic are myriad and as puzzling as a maze; the professional diplomat should be as competent as possible in the field.

Politics is the medium within which all the work of a diplomat must be cast; therefore, he must be familiar with its demands. In fact practice in the art for a time would furnish a good background. Then he would never be cynical about it; firsthand experience would show him that politics is a necessary mode of human action for which no substitute has ever been found. In a democracy it is a peculiarly vital kind of human action, for the politician is the broker who brings some element of consensus out of many conflicting attitudes and views. Indeed the politician exercises some of the same functions domestically that the diplomatist must perform internationally. Both must bring harmony from a wide diversity of interests and opinions. Unless the diplomat has a sympathetic, as well as an exact, understanding of political realities, he will be impatient with the Congress. The members of that body in their turn will be carping and censorious. Our history is strewn with examples of this truth. Under such emotional strains a diplomat, unhappy with his own government, cannot adequately represent the United States abroad.

The diplomat must also be a linguist. To Americans generally that seems a severe, even a harsh, demand. However, the block to linguistic competence is strictly psychological. Anyone who has traveled in Switzerland has met porters, waiters, and chauffeurs who speak four or five languages, yet make no pretense to learning, and regard themselves as laboring men. Languages can be mastered by people of modest talents if the effort seems to them worth while. No one should tackle diplomacy as a career who is not ready to meet that simple, but basic, challenge.

The diplomat must also be a man of the world, at least in the geographical sense. It is to his advantage to have traveled. In any event, he must be of a mind to travel; it should fascinate him. The late John Finley was an inveterate traveler physically, but he journeyed even more in his mind. He used to walk a great deal, but he made it a rule to travel intellectually at least ten miles every day. With maps and guide books he went over some area far more thoroughly than tourists on the ground would do. He knew many regions, their geological formations, their natural resources, their industries and arts, their people and customs. His imaginative travels were almost as rewarding as his actual visits to the same places; they made those pilgrimages more revealing and vivid. I am not suggesting that every budding diplomat should adopt the Finley habit. But he must have the kind of readiness to see and to learn, the kind of hospitality to foreign life and customs, which John Finley exhibited in such a superlative degree.

Some readers will by now have concluded that the diplomat must be a superman. It may seem to them that the qualities listed—not to speak of character, social grace, and personal magnetism—would require training so long that he would spend his life in learning and never arrive at the time to function. That is not true. Some of his education must be of a formal kind, acquired in school and college—and some perhaps by graduate work. Much of it—most of it, indeed—will be gained by experience and study while on the job.

If a person enters the Foreign Service at the usual age, he can expect thirty or forty years of official employment; that should be a period of continuous growth, his knowledge expanding as his responsibilities increase. Failure to manifest such growth should be the principal reason for "selection out" of the Service. Acquiring skill in diplomacy is a long and arduous business; it is not a "gift." One may have an aptitude, but it must be developed in the midst of the daily labor and all the other pressures which tend to reduce men to routinarians, which impair imagination and destroy the love of learning—better called "adventure."

3

The Early Record

The ideas of many people regarding American diplomacy belong to an age that is gone. It is quite customary for many to think of our diplomats in terms which were valid enough before the first World War, but have now ceased to correspond with the facts.

In 1914 Britain, France, and the United States were represented in eleven world centers, the eleventh in each instance being the home country. In the ten nations where Britain was represented abroad its chiefs of mission had an average of thirty-three years of professional experience; the French chiefs of mission in the ten capitals had over

thirty-four; the American ambassadors and ministers had
an average of a little less than one year of service in the field
of diplomacy. Needless to say, not a single one of the Americans was a professional diplomat. The year in which this
situation prevailed was significant—it was the year the first
World War broke out. Of course, these American amateurs
had professional help in their duties from other officers in
the embassies and legations, many or most of whom were
professionals. But the thinness and inadequacy of our representation at a moment of acute crisis are obvious. Our lack
of experienced diplomats was dramatically clear throughout
the first World War.

The interpretation of these historical facts will depend
upon the point of view of the commentator. Some are starkly
censorious, holding that our practices reflected negligence,
immaturity, or any one of a whole list of shortcomings
readily gleaned from the recent voluminous literature of
criticism. We have been blessed, if that is the word, with a
large number of flagellants, who feel an urge to mortify
themselves in print because the United States is what it is.
They harp upon the innate deficiencies of democracy, its
disadvantages in the formation and execution of policy, its
lack of clarity in statement and consistency in action. Some
seem to go almost as far as Thomas Carlyle, who said,
"Democracy is, by the nature of it, a self-cancelling business; and gives in the long run a net result of zero."

There is room for a different, and more optimistic, view.
The key to understanding how such a situation as existed
in our diplomatic establishment in 1914 came to pass lies not
in any record of failure but in earlier success in attaining a
goal long and ardently cherished. There was nothing inherent in the American system of government that accounted
for the lack of a large corps of professional diplomatists in

1914. It was not a measure of democracy's suspicion of the expert that produced this phenomenon.

For three quarters of a century or more the United States had enjoyed living in as much isolation as it desired. We had attained that desirable condition for which George Washington had called in his Farewell Address: "Europe has a set of primary interests which to us have none or a very remote relation. Hence ... it must be unwise in us to implicate ourselves by artificial ties in the ordinary vicissitudes of her politics or the ordinary combinations and collisions of her friendships or enmities."

It now requires a genuine effort at historical imagination to grasp the radical character of that proposition. Nearly three centuries had passed since America was discovered; through most of that long era its lands had been parceled and bartered, fought over and partitioned. It had been a kind of make-weight in the European balance of power. Washington was proposing a breach in historical continuity fully as severe as the separation from Britain. He was proposing to give independence a new dimension.

Our first President had adequate reason to realize that the break with Britain, symbolized by the Declaration of Independence and the Treaty of 1783, had not made us fully independent; Britain did not carry out the terms of the peace treaty for years. Other powers with an interest in what they called "legitimacy" were loath to recognize the revolutionary upstart. France, keenly aware of the part it had played in the success of our struggle, sent an envoy, Genêt, who obviously regarded the United States as a satellite; he had no hesitation in appealing directly to the people over the head of their government. So long as those things persisted, there were flaws in the concept of independence.

Worse perhaps, from Washington's point of view, was the blindness of some who could not see that only in strong union could those weaknesses in our status be cured. He was alert, therefore, to domestic dangers. He was sharply conscious of the fact that we were not a nation in the fullest sense, that the parochialisms and hostilities among the colonies had left residues of division that might split and destroy the unity of the new Republic. His Farewell Address reflects all these anxieties: "With me," he said, "a predominant motive has been to endeavor to gain time to our country to settle and mature its yet recent institutions and to progress without interruption to that degree of strength and consistency which is necessary to give it, humanly speaking, the command of its own fortunes."

He did not live to see the achievement of his cherished objective—full independence from Europe. But it was attained, and in larger measure than he could have foreseen. The preoccupation of Europe with the Napoleonic Wars, the disruption of its "concert of powers," our acquisition of Louisiana and Florida, the independence of Latin America from Spain and Portugal, the enunciation of the Monroe Doctrine, the check to Russia on the West Coast—all these and other events combined to put the United States in the happy international situation of independent isolation for which Washington had longed.

Thus by 1835 Alexis de Tocqueville could describe the position of the United States in these terms: "The United States is a nation without neighbors. Separated from the rest of the world by the ocean, and too weak as yet to aim at dominion of the seas, it has no enemies, and its interests rarely come into contact with those of any other nation of the globe." "The policy of the Americans in relation to the whole world is exceedingly simple; and it may almost be said that nobody stands in need of them, nor do they stand in need of anybody. Their independence is never threatened. . . . nothing is to be feared from the pressure of external dangers."

Freedom from contact with foreign countries did not go so far as some members of the First Congress had anticipated; they felt that after we had made treaties of commerce and friendship with the leading nations we would not need representation abroad except through consuls, and there would not be enough work for a Department of Foreign Affairs. That is why other duties of a domestic character were added and the name of the first department was changed to Department of State.

As late as 1801 Thomas Jefferson continued to hope for some such situation. Writing to William Short in Paris, the President said: "We wish to let every treaty we have drop off without renewal. We call in our diplomatic missions, barely keeping up those to the most important nations. There is a strong disposition in our countrymen to discontinue even these; and very possibly it may be done. Consuls will be continued as usual." Though such expectations could not permanently be realized, the isolation actually attained was remarkable both in degree and in kind.

One obvious, but no less important, conclusion arises from this historic fact of the attainment of Washington's goal: neither an important nor interesting career was available for American professional diplomats. It is captious to be critical of the "failure" to create a professional corps when there was no adequate outlet for its talents and energies. To assert that the needs of the twentieth century should have been foreseen is to expect what politics never does—either in a democracy or any other form of government.

The reasoning which leads to the conclusion that the absence of a professional corps of diplomats arose from the international position of the United States, rather than from deficiencies attributable to its democratic character, is based on powerful evidence from earlier history.

In colonial and revolutionary days, in Washington's administration and afterward until that larger measure of independence had been realized, we used professional diplomats. Some of them were exceedingly influential men in our early history. Every President between Washington and Jackson had diplomatic experience: John Adams, Thomas Jefferson, James Monroe, John Quincy Adams all served in diplomatic posts abroad and three of them served also as Secretaries of State. James Madison was the only President during that era who had not held a European diplomatic post, but he was Secretary of State for eight years, and was thoroughly familiar with problems in foreign affairs. Washington, himself, was so profoundly impressed with the importance of foreign relations that he personally read all the previous correspondence, making careful notes in the margin to help fix the record in his memory.

This is not the only evidence of the seriousness with which diplomacy was regarded in the days when the United States was trying to establish its real, complete independence. Most people are astonished at the historical comment of the late Carl Russell Fish: "Of men trained in the more essential elements of diplomacy the colonies had a greater proportion than any other country of the time." Officers and agents of the colonies engaged in negotiations with the Indians, occasionally with the French and Spanish, a great deal with each other, and continuously with the British government. These quasi-diplomatic officials were not, indeed, sticklers for protocol. They had a certain scorn for the fusty conventions which had made negotiation sometimes as formal and com-

plicated as a gavotte. But of the substance of the matter
they had a firm grasp.

Benjamin Franklin was a sensational success in France.
Often descriptions of his dress and his methods have created
the impression that he was an amateur brilliantly holding
his own against the professionals by the force and charm of
his personality, his wit, and his intellect. He was, indeed, an
original, unique. Nevertheless, he was also trained in just
the way that has been suggested as essential for today. He
had a wide-ranging mind, catholic interests and tastes; he
had traveled and had learned. He lived abroad almost con-
tinually for sixteen years before the Revolution as general
agent for various colonies and groups of colonies. With the
outbreak of the Revolution he was sent to Montreal in an
effort to induce the Canadians to join the new Republic,
and he was later appointed to a commission to listen to
General Howe's peace proposals. For years, therefore, he
had been performing the kind of duties he was later to
perform for the Republic during his nine years in France
after the Declaration of Independence. To think of him as
an amateur is to misread history. The same could be said
with equal truth of John Adams, his son John Quincy
Adams, Thomas Jefferson, and several others.

The seriousness with which diplomacy was taken in the
early days is further evidenced by its fiscal importance. Soon
after the proclamation of neutrality of 1793 (itself a remarkable landmark in modern diplomacy), at a time when the
whole expense of the new Federal government was less than
ten million dollars, Congress appropriated a million dollars
"to defray any expenses which may be incurred in relation
to the intercourse between the United States and foreign
nations." In 1806, when we were caught in a cleft stick between Napoleon's Decrees and Britain's Orders in Council,

an appropriation of two million was voted—more than a fifth of the total authorized expenditure of the whole government. If we were to spend a proportionate amount today on the Department of State, the Foreign Service, the International Cooperation Agency, and the United States Information Agency, it would amount to many times present appropriations even if we included every form of aid.

It would be possible to continue piling up historical evidence. Surely, however, there is no need to do so; it must be amply clear that when diplomacy had a vital role to play in the life of the American nation it was treated appropriately; there was a marked effort to choose men of talent and experience for its tasks.

Pessimists regarding the capacity of the American democracy to use professionals would argue that the historical evidence, accurate as it is, is hardly relevant. They would invite attention to the fact that the United States was not then a mass democracy in the current sense, and that public opinion did not exercise so close a supervision over foreign affairs as is the case today. They hold that the structure and functioning of the government itself have changed so much in size and in other respects that it is essentially different in character from the government which existed from the days of Washington through the administration of John Quincy Adams.

Both points deserve a word of comment. The concept of democracy has indeed made giant strides; the suffrage has been vastly extended. Yet there is another factor to be stressed. Relative to the means of communication and opportunities for information, the public in those early years followed—and influenced—foreign policy in a very marked degree. The enthusiasm displayed for Genêt, the heat engendered by Jay's treaty, the tension over the Alien and

Sedition Acts, the excitement over Jefferson's diplomacy, and dozens of other instances make it sufficiently apparent that public opinion was alert, and that it was an important, sometimes a dominant, factor in shaping policy.

Furthermore, that "Democracy of the Elite" (or however current critics of modern democracy choose to describe it) was sometimes as "wrong" in its judgments on particular issues and at specific moments as the critics assert the mass democracy of our time to have been. Washington never would have voiced his arguments with such fervor in his Farewell Address if he had not been keenly aware of the significance of public sentiment and of the sharp divisions of opinion regarding our proper course of action. When he wrote, "if we remain one nation," the words meant just what they said—a real doubt lest the Union should not endure. As we read the words today, we tend to slur over them without noticing their significance. When he used such words as "I conjure you to believe me," he was choosing language much more urgent than was his wont. And he was appealing to public opinion.

Inferences properly to be drawn from the assertion that the structure of government was then quite different can vary markedly from those of the pessimists regarding our capacity to use professionals in diplomacy. It is true that there have been great changes in the operation of our government. That is true of the governments of all nations, virtually without exception. It is fair to say, too, that as compared with other nations the government of the United States has always been extraordinarily flexible. The written Constitution was not designed as a strait jacket and it has not proved to be one. There have been sharp, even decisive, changes. The vital role of parties, for example, was not foreseen nor planned by the framers of the Constitution, yet

parties were found to be essential and became the driving
force of the machinery of government. The Jeffersonian and
Jacksonian "revolutions" were easily contained within Constitutional limits. The silent revolution by which the Speaker
of the House became dominant could take place almost
unnoticed.

Woodrow Wilson in his first book, *Congressional Government,* asserted that the "Congress is fast becoming the governing body of the nation." The powers of the executive did
not impress him any more than, two generations before, they
had impressed de Tocqueville, who wrote that "in all his
important acts" the President "is directly or indirectly subject to the legislature, and of his own free authority he can
do but little." "He is not . . . a part of the sovereign power,
but only its agent. . . . The President is placed beside the
legislature like an inferior and dependent power." The young
Wilson spoke of "the declining prestige of the presidential
office"; "its power has waned." Moreover, cabinet members
seemed to him to be "in the leading strings of statutes, and
all their duties look towards a strict obedience to Congress."
By the time he published the fifteenth edition of *Congressional Government* in 1900—fifteen years after the first
edition—he saw evidence of some emergence of the Presidency, a movement his own administration was vastly to
accelerate.

Thus, within broad limits, the flexibility of our government is astonishing. It is not surprising, therefore, that the
use of experienced diplomats should decline to the point of
disappearance when our independence was fully established
and we had attained the "suitable establishments" for "a
respectably defensive posture" for which Washington argued.
Diplomacy was no longer concerned with great issues; foreign affairs declined from a dominant to a subordinate posi-

tion. The subjects to which we confined our interposition internationally were not such as to challenge the interests and talents of the ablest and most ambitious men.

First-class men want to deal with first-class events—and for three-quarters of a century those were domestic, not foreign. The advent of the spoils system in all its initial dominance merely accentuated a trend away from professional diplomats. The long period—almost to the end of the nineteenth century—of effective isolation was certain to set patterns regarding professionals that would require years to alter.

4

Progress to the Modern Era

After so long an era of virtual isolation the change to a new reliance upon experts and professionals was bound to be gradual. The return toward the use of career officers in diplomacy began, modestly, even before the first World War. It appeared in embryo during the 1890's, when the United States was beginning to think of itself in terms of a world power.

In 1893, for the first time, the appropriations for the support of our representatives abroad contemplated that we might have ambassadors, the highest grade possible, in some diplomatic posts. Though the Constitution had specifically

mentioned ambassadors, we had been content for nearly a
century and a quarter to designate a minister as our highest
diplomatic officer. That was a clear reflection of our limited
role in world affairs and of our view of ourselves as less than
a first-class power. In 1894 the legations in Great Britain,
France, Russia, and Germany were raised to embassies; that
act symbolized a new concept of our position in the world.

Development of our world status was hastened and accentuated by the dramatic events which clustered about the
year 1898—the Spanish-American War, our acquisition of
Puerto Rico and the Philippines, dominance over Cuba, the
annexation of Hawaii and Samoa, the position we took with
regard to the Integrity of China and the Open Door. A whole
spate of activities around the turn of the century brought the
United States upon the world stage in a manner that had
not been customary during the preceding seventy-five years.
Relative to our current activities these stirrings may not
seem of great moment. But they produced violent public
controversy and were early harbingers of the end of isolation.

During this period, also, our commercial position in the
world scheme of things was rising steadily. Consequently
the consular system, which had been fee-supported and had
long been the prey of the spoilsmen, was put upon a merit
basis. The accomplishment was bipartisan in character. In
1895 President Cleveland issued an executive order which
is historically decisive as a turning point. It provided that
consular vacancies should be filled by transfer or promotion
from some other position under the Department of State of
a nature tending to qualify the incumbent for consular work,
or by someone who had previously served satisfactorily in
the Department of State, or by a person with adequate
character and responsibility who passed a competitive examination.

This change in practice at the consular level, launched by executive order, was later made permanent by statute in 1906. Members of the consular service were classified into several groups and the various posts were graded. The whole was firmly and finally established upon a merit basis; the spoils system was eliminated. The statute was implemented by executive orders issued by President Theodore Roosevelt; he filled in the details of the examination, the methods of appointment and promotion.

Today we have a professional consular service and have had for over half a century. Consular officers have not been so well paid as they should have been; they have not had the recognition they deserved; but there is, and has long been, a sound professional basis for the whole system. Pessimists regarding the capacity of a democracy to use professional diplomatists may grant the accuracy of that statement; they demur at its importance by asserting that consuls do not perform diplomatic functions; they do not constitute an "elite corps." Of course major negotiations do not lie in their hands; nevertheless, their importance in our relations abroad should not, for that reason, be underestimated.

They are scattered about over the world, not concentrated in capital cities only. They are in a position to observe aspects of provincial life with which embassies have little contact, yet which profoundly affect relationships among peoples. They are the sources of many kinds of economic and commercial information, and, as has been emphasized, this may involve political consequences, sometimes of a high order of importance. Moreover, inasmuch as the Foreign Service has not been divided into two separate groups, consular and diplomatic, since 1924, the training a man receives in the provincial cities as a consul often stands him in good stead in his subsequent diplomatic assignments.

For these and other reasons, the long and sound tradition of professionals in the consular field can be dangerously discounted. Some of the ablest of our older professional diplomats were consuls before the services became amalgamated. Some of the younger men now arriving at posts of high responsibility have had valuable consular experience since the union of the two branches.

So far as the diplomatic service is concerned, it grew virtually without notice at first. As business increased abroad, young men went, principally upon the basis of personal acquaintance or family friendship, to be secretaries to the ministers and ambassadors of the United States. Some enjoyed the service because it was interesting socially; others found it intellectually rewarding. They tended, therefore, to stay on after the men who had appointed them were replaced or resigned. Thus there developed a group of apprentices, eager to make a career of diplomacy and ready to undertake its hazards without any security of a statutory kind or, at the beginning, even the security of an executive order. Some of them rose to distinction, among others John Hay, W. W. Rockhill, and Henry White.

In 1909 President Taft took cognizance of this whole situation; he did for the diplomatic service below the rank of chief of mission what Cleveland had done for the consular service. By executive order he gave civil service status to the various grades of secretary of legation or embassy. He also directed the Secretary of State to call to the attention of the President from time to time those professionals who showed such skill and maturity in their work as to be worthy of promotion to the rank of chief of mission.

This was an extraordinary step; it removed the ceiling over promotion and set up a systematic basis for a corps of professional diplomatists. Such a decisive change had collateral effects of great importance; for example, its operation upon any rational plan required the maintenance of an efficiency record in the Department of State. Upon this record a man could be promoted, transferred, or dropped from the Service. Despite all the vicissitudes of subsequent years, that record still remains the keystone of the whole system; it still furnishes the data for promotion from one grade to the next, or for detachment from the Service. With the passage of time criteria have been more sharply defined, procedures have been elaborated; none of these refinements has altered the basic reliance on a cumulative efficiency record.

President Taft's executive order further provided that those who were appointed from outside the Service should come only into the lower grades, that vacancies in the higher classes were to be filled exclusively by promotion. Moreover, entrance to the lowest grade thereafter was to be by competitive examination. Thus a young man no longer needed to have connections of an influential character in order to undertake a career in the Foreign Service.

It was inevitable after this program had been launched by executive order that it should be codified and made more stable by statute. This was done early in 1915. That date is suggestive; it was soon after the outbreak of war in Europe had dramatized the inadequacy of our existing diplomatic representation. Thereafter all appointments of secretaries in the diplomatic service and consuls were to be made by commission to the offices of secretary of embassy or legation, or consul, and not by commission to any particular post. This made it possible for the Secretary of State to assign officers to different posts and transfer them from one to another with a high degree of flexibility. The act also set up classes and salaries for each class; there were five classes of secretaries of legation or embassy, five classes of consuls general, and nine classes of consuls.

Moreover, this early statute contained a vitally important provision: secretaries of embassy and consuls were to be brought home from time to time and assigned to duty in the Department of State without loss of grade or salary. The objective was to give them an opportunity to refresh their awareness and understanding of what was happening at home and to see how policy was made.

This provision for "re-Americanization" has sometimes caused heartburning, and the term, in particular, is resented. Nevertheless, the procedure is fundamental, and has a long historical background. Thomas Jefferson had a firsthand experience which convinced him of its necessity: "When I returned from France, after an absence of 6. or 7. years, I was astonished at the change which I found had taken place. . . . I . . . found myself not at all qualified to speak their sentiments, or forward their views." He wrote to a fellow diplomat: "We return like foreigners, &, like them, require a considerable residence here to become Americanized." "Very soon, therefore, after entering on the office of Sec. of State, I recommended to Gen. Washington to establish as a rule of practice, that no person should be continued on foreign mission beyond an absence of 6., 7., or 8. years. He approved it."

Modern communications have made so rigid a rule much less necessary. Nonetheless, Jefferson's observations of himself and other American diplomats developed a sound point of view and every statute since the professional diplomatic service was organized has embodied some provision for this "re-Americanization." The latest act, that of 1946, specifically requires every Foreign Service officer to spend at least three years of his first fifteen in this country. Unhappily, the essential assignment to the Department of State was allowed to fall almost into disuse in the years immediately after the second World War. It occurred, so far as can be observed, not because of any conscious change of policy, but through sheer administrative ineptitude.

This somewhat technical historical review has a deep significance for our topic. It makes it perfectly clear that, as our position matured in the international world, we set about the alteration of the organization and structure of our consular and diplomatic representation to accord with that changing position. In short, as soon as national interest made a professional service seem of vital importance, the spoils system was thrust into the background and the merit system (which is simply another phrase to describe a professional service) was brought to the fore.

Perfectionists and pessimists will join in the assertion that the development of the Foreign Service did not keep pace with the need. Of course, more speed would have been desirable. But what evidence is there that any other form of government would have done better? The reason the British and French were ahead of us in the matter of professional diplomacy in 1914 is self evident: they had been "world powers" much longer than we. But even though Britain was ahead of us in consolidating the Foreign Office and the diplomatic service, it was slower than the United States in joining consular and diplomatic officers into a single professional corps. In 1943 the British incorporated their commercial attachés into the foreign service, as the United States had already done in 1939. All the great powers now have adopted the principle of a united foreign service.

In our present hindsight, the President did not establish the merit system as rapidly as might have been desirable.

But the Executive cannot move too far ahead of public sentiment, else he will be checked in his course; he can move only as fast as public opinion will tolerate. In other forms of government checks upon the initiative of heads of states may not be equally obvious, but it is a gross error to suppose that any chief of state has a free hand. If he is not controlled by public opinion, it will be by a palace clique, or some other group. There is nothing in recorded history that justifies the assumption that the bureaucracy inherent in totalitarianism is any more alert to changing needs than public opinion in a democracy.

What is abundantly clear, and of transcendant importance, is the rapidity with which events of the first World War taught the United States the necessity for a professional service. Equally impressive is the speed with which members of the Service then rose to posts of great influence. When the Harding administration took office, except for the Secretary himself, all the chief officers of the Department of State were professionals. The Under Secretary and two of the three Assistant Secretaries were Foreign Service officers, as were the chiefs of most of the geographic bureaus. The Second Assistant Secretary was the redoubtable Alvey A. Adee, a professional career Departmental officer, as was a Fourth Assistant Secretary, promoted to that office after its creation by the Rogers Act of 1924.

It is particularly significant, moreover, that the basic reform, which united all our official representatives abroad into one service, was passed in 1924. The Rogers Act became law at a time when we had rejected membership in the League of Nations, when we were not entering the World Court, and soon after the late President had talked of "normalcy," hoping for some return to isolation. Those were manifestations of a mood of reaction. But they did not deflect the progress toward a united professional Foreign Service Officer corps. By uniting the two personnel systems and unifying their control, opportunities were provided for people to develop in ways that had not been possible since the days of John Quincy Adams. The Rogers Act supplied the Secretary of State with a far more powerful instrument for the implementation of policy than had been in existence for a century or more before that time.

It is unnecessary to detail the vicissitudes of the Service since 1924. They have been many. In general its difficulties have reflected lack of administrative interest on the part of successive Secretaries of State more than anything else. When one considers the range and complexity, not to mention the sheer bulk, of current business in a foreign office, it is astonishing to find how few Secretaries have appreciated the need for sound administration in order adequately to exploit the talents available in the serried ranks of experts within the Department.

It was a tragic error, for example, to suspend all recruitment to the Service during the war. This was part of a false supposition that nothing counts but force, that wars are won only on the battlefields, and that "unconditional surrender" can somehow be the equivalent of peace. It was part of the underestimation of the fact that when the fighting is done the struggle for peace is just begun. The slightest appreciation of history would show that a "dictated" peace is no peace at all.

Woodrow Wilson had that in mind when he used the unfortunate phrase "peace without victory"; later he was more explicit when he said that a dictated peace "accepted in humiliation . . . would leave a sting, a resentment, a bitter memory upon which terms of peace would rest, not permanently, but only upon quicksand." The reality, demonstrated again and again, is that every peace must in the long run be a negotiated peace, and satisfactory not alone to the victor but to the defeated. All that is as clear as daylight now, but it was obscured by the heat of strife, and the inability of men in office to subordinate their passions to their intelligence.

Lack of appreciation of the essentiality of sound administrative practices led to the serious mistake of having nine or ten administrators of the Department of State within a decade. The operation of so vast an enterprise requires experience and knowledge, and the kind of understanding that comes only with time. None of the administrative heads had time enough to master the routines; instead the routines controlled them; the sheer weight of the bureaucratic machinery proved suffocating to men who were not in office long enough to dominate it.

It was also a grave error to set up so many agencies outside the Department, and then to show so much instability in their location and their functions. This was done by Presidents who were, themselves, not interested in organization, who discounted the necessity for skilled, expert career services. It seemed sometimes that disorganization was intentional, in order to avoid delegating authority. One reorganization followed another in far too rapid succession, and the names of agencies were changed with almost whimsical nonchalance.

These errors were not the result of wrong views on the part of the public; they were mistakes which arose from a leadership which depended too much upon inspiration, and too little on preparation. A learned and temperate British commentator wrote of President Roosevelt's conduct of foreign policy as "personal and untidy," reducing the State Department to a "cipher . . . during the latter part of Mr.

Cordell Hull's tenure and the incumbency of Mr. Stettinius."

The fault was not presidential alone; our Secretaries of State hoped to think great thoughts and develop great policies without realizing their necessary dependence upon advisers and staff workers and people who have to implement them. Secretaries insisted on loading current business on the Policy Planning Staff; they declined to follow the recommendation of the Hoover Commission that its energies should be turned to the forward planning that its name implies. None of these errors is inherent within the democratic structure of our government. They reflect unfortunate personal idiosyncrasies of officials.

Some Foreign Service officers were not without blame. A group of seasoned members of the corps were responsible for writing into the Foreign Service Act of 1946 a provision that a director general, drawn from their own number, should manage the Service. This could deprive the Secretary, in some critical situation, of the power to administer a vital part of the Department for whose operation he is responsible. It violated the sound principle that the chief political officer should have real, not formal, control. Upon the recommendation of the first Hoover Commission, of which Secretary Acheson was vice chairman, the Congress returned the power of control to the Secretary. It is not using too strong language to say that some influential senior officers sulked over this, and damaged needlessly the morale of their own Service.

Central to our thought amid all the confusions of recent discussion should be the remembrance that the Foreign Service not only survived; it grew in experience and maturity. We have today both the best trained and the best disciplined diplomatic service in all our history; it is as good as any in the world. There are men of high ability in many posts around the world and young men coming up through the Service who will mature into professional diplomats of the very first order of capacity.

There are shortcomings and deficiencies to which I have given attention in other contexts. Some of these are in process of reform; indeed it is not too much to say that the current effort at reform is the greatest that has been undertaken in thirty years. Even these reforms have the defects of compromise, and the shortcomings of clumsy administrative machinery. But perfection eludes most governmental efforts.

Certainly no series of administrative errors can conceal the dramatic change since 1914. Then not a single one of our missions in the great capitals had a professional at its head; today over two-thirds of our missions abroad have professional chiefs. In some of the most important positions, such as Moscow, a professional is ambassador, and serving with brilliant skill. In enormously sensitive areas, such as India, the Middle East, and Japan, we have in recent years had, as chiefs of mission, professionals who have done magnificent work for us.

Congress has seen how important is the professional service and recently, without controversy, established the grade of career ambassador—a striking symbol of fresh recognition of the status attained by the Foreign Service. Many high posts in the Department of State are occupied by seasoned veterans of the career group, and as a consequence of current reforms many more such positions will be available to them.

A review of the history of the United States and the relationship which the democratic structure of our government bears to diplomacy demonstrates that the determining factors in creating a career service have been the status of this nation in the world and the estimates of its situation on the part of the public. Whenever and wherever diplomacy has become a matter of first importance to the national survival, we have developed professionals to help us over each crisis. In the early days of the Republic the need was met; at that time there were men of talents, indeed of brilliance, for whom diplomacy became a major interest in their careers. It ought to be added that there were also men of modest ability, and, as always, some whose characters did not measure up to the strain put upon them.

This last fact warrants emphasis, for we do our nation no service by making our forefathers into demigods. That is a historical distortion amounting to falsification, and defeats any judicious appraisal of the current scene. It is worth while to remind ourselves that glorification of the past is a characteristic human fault against which we must guard. "There were giants in the earth in those days" is a phrase that occurs in the sixth chapter of the Book of Genesis. At the dawn of recorded history men were already looking back upon the great men of an already dim past. It requires a special effort to remember that the heroes of the early Republic were human, and not all the actors in the great revolutionary drama were heroes, by any means.

As at the beginning, so later when the United States emerged from isolation and entered upon what Herbert Croly, nearly fifty years ago, called a "career in the world," there again began to emerge a group of career diplomats. The two developments did not keep exact pace with each other; in human affairs that never happens. Nonetheless, the professional service did keep within measurable distance of our responsibilities. Failure to narrow the gap was due neither to deficiencies inherent in democracy nor to structural faults in our government. It was the result of personal characteristics of officials who either lacked administrative capacity or underestimated the importance of that kind of talent.

Now that we have been cast in the role of major partner within the great Western alliance and one of the principal spokesmen for democracy, the future of the professional diplomat is assured. Public opinion will tolerate no return to the spoils system, nor any diminution of the influence of the professional. We shall construct a larger and even sounder corps of career men and women who give their lives to diplomacy in the service of democracy.

5

Other Nations

The historical experience of the United States is adequate
to destroy the argument that democracy is more hostile to
professionals in diplomacy than other types of government.
It equally refutes the contention that the structure of our
government is incompatible with the development of a
corps of professional diplomatists. There is inherent in the
negativism of the pessimists an implication that some other
nation handles the matter better than does the United
States. If that were not implied, the criticism would be such
patent nonsense as to get no hearing at all. If no other
government does better, the difficulties must be characteristic of diplomacy itself.

Where shall we turn to find a model system which does not share the deficiencies which seem so striking to current critics of the United States system? Japan, in the days before the war, was not a democracy, so that its diplomatic service was free of that "handicap." It had a parliamentary form of government, so the tensions between the executive and the legislative that pessimists find so disheartening in our structure of government were lacking. The Japanese certainly had a well trained corps of professionals at their disposal; they were adept in every technique of the craft. Was their policy, therefore, more coherent; was it pursued with greater singleness of purpose—or more success—than those of the Western democracies? Were their diplomatists encouraged to report with candor views differing from those held by the foreign office, or was some measure of conformity essential for promotion?

In perspective, nothing is clearer than the fact that the Japanese system, as it was developed in the first half of the twentieth century, led directly to complete disaster. It was never in the national interest of Japan to challenge so directly the settled policies of the United States and Britain; it was never in their interest to make the ties with Hitler and to participate in the second World War. Lack of democratic checks upon the action of public officers gave the military too much authority. Indeed, it was the military clique which was able to alter an American communication in order to precipitate war. Surely, in the light of what actually happened, no critic of the American system will propose pre-war Japan as a model.

It is beyond belief that anyone would seriously advance the idea that Mussolini's Italy or Hitlerite Germany could supply us with a pattern of professional diplomacy in accordance with which we might shape our own action. Perhaps the diplomatists employed by the Soviets are in the minds of the critics. They have had a series of professionals of redoubtable skill—Litvinov, Molotov, Gromyko, Vishinsky, and many others. Soviet policy is defined by the ruling group and obedience to its mandates is enforced through rigorous discipline. Of these things there can be no doubt. True their policy at one moment seems contradictory to equally specific past policy, but that is because the zigzag technique is employed so ardently.

Yet in our present mood of defeatism in the presence of Soviet penetration, when any expression of optimism by the Secretary of State is denounced as misleading, we may have lost perspective. Wendell Willkie on his globe-circling effort to discover "One World" found that we had a reservoir of good will which could be drained; was it not also true that at war's end the Soviets had won the admiration of the world by their courage at Stalingrad and elsewhere? Did not their international behavior—their diplomacy—thereafter bring them to a very low estate in world opinion by the time Stalin died?

By repudiating, first implicitly, then explicitly at the Party Congress this winter, much of what they had done and defended, by denouncing the man to whom they had so long toadied, they displayed "flexibility." In the present defeatist mood about democracy, every Russian act of tergiversation seems to appear as a triumph of this vaunted flexibility. But there is another valid view: a recent writer suggests that the new leaders may "have broken the tablets of orthodoxy which held the whole communist myth together." The Soviet blessing of Jugoslavia's nationalist "deviation," whose success (with Western help) forced reversal of policy upon the Presidium, may have let the giant Nationalism out of the Stalinist bottle. This action may show "flexibility," it may show "realism," but those are short-term judgments. The long-run effect may be to oblige the Soviets to maintain their coalition by consent, like the voluntarism of the Western alliance, with all the divisions and tensions that change would involve.

Whether under the old dispensation or the new, does anyone suggest that Soviet diplomatists are models, or that their system has anything to recommend it? Decision making is simplified, surely; coherence in statement at any given moment is attained—without doubt. But the diplomatists are errand boys who spread honey one moment and poison the next at a command from on high. Smiles that are thin at best are replaced by scowls that are synthetic. Is such technical skill as several of these diplomats have displayed a substitute for integrity? I doubt seriously that the critics want to adopt all the "advantages" the Soviets possess.

Perhaps the British have the answer, as has often been suggested by those who see defects arising from the "structure" of our government. There is one flaw in the suggestion, for the United Kingdom, like the United States, is a democracy. Therefore, if democracy is the barrier, if, as one critic believes, "the people have acquired power which they are incapable of exercising, and the governments they elect have lost power which they must recover if they are to govern," then Britain is no better off than are we. In that case there is no need to examine its experience with professional diplomats.

If, however, the fault is with the structure of our government, perhaps British experience would be worth consideration. There is no such breach between the executive and the legislative as we know, no checks and balances. For the Prime Minister and his Cabinet are all in Parliament, and cannot be repudiated by Parliament without precipitating an election in which the ousters may themselves be ousted. There is, moreover, much stronger party discipline than exists in the United States. It is evident that both these circumstances make for coherence and consistency, if those are the most precious jewels of diplomacy.

Furthermore, the British cannot, by any stretch of terminology, be called "immature." The United Kingdom is not newly come to the world stage; its classic support of the Balance of Power is among the oldest and most persistently pursued of all foreign policies. From time to time Britain has shown so much "flexibility" as to give currency, long ago, to the phrase, "perfidious Albion." But flexibility has survived; it would be difficult, for instance, to find in all history such a reversal of position as led to the change from Empire to Commonwealth. The successive steps were not perfectly timed; hindsight makes that plain. Nevertheless, the timing was better than that of the French, or the Dutch, for example.

With all this change there is an element of stability, or at least continuity. Its Foreign Office has a "Permanent" Under Secretary, a professional who exercises great influence upon policy. Americans should be reminded that, as in everything political, there is an element of relativity in the word "Permanent." In the first place it refers to the office, not the man; the incumbent seldom serves more than four or five years, usually at the end of his career. Moreover, the Permanent Under Secretary can be removed at any time. The classic instance was the dismissal of Lord Vansittart by Neville Chamberlain. Far from being a breach of propriety, Vansittart himself declared that it was the right thing to do since their views of the correct policy to pursue were so fundamentally at variance that effective collaboration was impossible.

The episode highlighted a basic fact which underlies the use of professional experts not only in foreign affairs, but in every other field—military, scientific, cultural, informational: the political officer must have the last word. The expert must be allowed to lay his views candidly before his political superior; those expressions of opinion should have the fullest and most careful consideration, but the politician, to use the least popular term, must take the final action and assume responsibility for it. In this respect the British situation is not so greatly different from ours as sometimes appears.

Too often it is assumed that the Permanent Under Secretary is the top officer of the Foreign Office save only for the Secretary of State for Foreign Affairs. While he does have direct access to the Foreign Secretary, there are no less than seven political officers in the top echelon of policy making. Besides the Foreign Secretary there are two Ministers of State, one in the Commons and one in the Lords; there are two Parliamentary Under Secretaries in the Commons; in addition both the Secretary and the Minister of State have Parliamentary private secretaries in the Commons. This is a heavier political top layer than we normally have in the United States.

Moreover, an inspection of their governmental reports on the Foreign Service is revealing. It shows that, despite their longer diplomatic history, and in spite of the traditional dignity and importance of the professional civil servant, the same problems have dogged the British as have harassed us.

There is another myth about their professional diplomatists that needs to be exploded. In its truly professional stage the British Foreign Service is not so much older than our own as is usually supposed. As we have seen, the beginnings of our organized and safeguarded professional service belong to the early years of this century. The British career diplomatic service was the product of the later years of the nineteenth century. Moreover, it was not until after the first World War, after the Diplomatic Service and the Foreign Office had been amalgamated, that its function of supplying expert advice to the Secretary was fully developed.

In the classic days of nineteenth century diplomacy the Foreign Office was essentially clerical. The transition to its new advisory status was gradual; indeed it was somewhat too gradual. In the twenties, and even more seriously in the thirties, its experts were brushed off. Prime Ministers Stanley Baldwin and Neville Chamberlain turned to Treasury officials rather than the Foreign Office for counsel. "There was a gap between Foreign Office expert knowledge and the Cabinet decisions of the time and public opinion in the country at large. . . . The knowledge and advice of the Foreign Office did not get across to the Government. And during the disastrous nineteen thirties the gap often became a chasm."

In some matters of organization Great Britain has not been much, if any, ahead of the United States. It was not until after the "Eden Reforms" of 1943 that the consular service, the commercial diplomatic service, and the information service were fused into the Foreign Service.

Even these reforms did not produce complete satisfaction. Last fall the *Manchester Guardian,* certainly a respected journal, published a series of articles on the British Foreign Service. It is no less than astonishing to see how close was the parallel with our difficulties and perplexities. Their service, like our own, "believed itself suspected by a large part of the public," especially after the defection of Burgess and Maclean in 1951. "It is often represented as inefficient and overpaid, divided into cliques, out of touch with the times, ignorant of the countries with which it is supposed to deal, spending its time at cocktail parties, meeting the wrong people, obsessed with pension prospects, its members bound together in a trade union whose main rule is that all should stand defensively together against the public and that the inefficient and unworthy should never be heavily penalized."

The articles discussed the effort to "democratise" the service, and the amalgamation of the diplomatic, consular, and commercial services. They reviewed the hoary argument, so familiar in this country, about "generalists" and "specialists," and the problems of in-service training to assure particular competence for particular areas, as, for example, the Far East. They printed the criticism, so often heard in this country, that not enough room is made for expert economists. They presented the difficulties of recruiting new members in terms familiar here, pointed out the hardships of living at home where allowances are inadequate, and described the manner in which that leads officers to eschew assignments in London, as ours do in Washington. Details concerning promotions, their pace, their justice and all the factors familiar here were there repeated. The "creaking machinery" of coordinating policy at home and abroad, and between the two, appeared as evident in Whitehall as in Foggy Bottom.

It seems reasonably clear that one cannot look abroad to find a model upon which to give assurance that we— or they—can have diplomatists as well as diplomats, men who devote their lives effectively and with public appreciation to representation of the national interest internationally.

These things being so, what moves the critics to their pronounced pessimism? Strangely enough it is nostalgia.

They look back upon a time before the people "acquired power which they are incapable of exercising," to an age when "a country's relations with its neighbors or with distant lands were dealt with almost exclusively by the head of of the State—Emperor, King or President—acting with the more-or-less dependent Minister-of-State, who was not representative of the masses, but the employé of the Monarch." "The principle of the system was . . . that war and peace were the business of the executive department. The power of decision was not in, was not even shared with, the House of Commons, the Chamber of Deputies, the Reichstag."

Mass democracy, on the contrary, "would not think" and "would not allow their leaders to think"; "the general rule is that a democratic politician had better not be right too soon." "This devitalization of the governing power is the malady of democratic states"; in that sentence "governing power" means the executive.

All this involves a condensation, and an interpretation, of history which are no less than astounding. It asserts that the "age of progress" ended just when the span of life was extended by ten or twenty years through the medical arts; when educational and cultural opportunities were available—and employed—on a scale unknown in those halcyon days when the Monarch ruled; when facilities for seeing the world were available and enjoyed by more people every year than moved in any of the great migrations of history; when the burdens of drudgery and the worse burdens of discrimination were being lifted from women; when racial prejudice was being systematically attacked and overcome; when science and technology were creating new marvels. The progress accomplished since the end of "the age of progress" makes that era seem puny.

Actually those halcyon days never existed. "Every successive generation tends to take its own troubles seriously, even tragically, and to feel that it is on the brink of calamity. . . . The memoirs of nineteenth century statesmen are full of anxieties and forebodings about foreign affairs; and the reasons they had were neither unreal nor unsubstantial."

There never was a government of "wise men"; Plato was expounding a great human desire; it can be compared with the eternal longing for peace. But the Monarchs did not keep the peace; and domestically they resorted to inflation more than have the democracies. Moreover, the earlier British Foreign Secretaries, operating without the pressures of as much Parliamentary scrutiny as now, and without dominant public opinion, were blind to economic and fiscal problems which could have been handled more readily before they grew so great. One of the expert departmental officials hammered away for seventeen years to make this point, but without avail. There was crass and, sad to say, deliberate ignorance regarding the people in colonies and dependent areas, for which the free world is now paying a bitter price. With the perfect 20-20 vision of hindsight it is easy to see how myopic the "great diplomatists" were in some matters, and how astigmatic in others. These were the men who did not have to face "hard problems."

There is no hope and no guidance in nostalgia; no one would recreate *all* the conditions that existed. To assert that in the midst of the Industrial Revolution and the Agricultural Revolution, not to speak of those in communications, "governments rarely had to make hard decisions" is historical nonsense. It was before "the people" took charge that the statesmen brought on the first World War, for it is asserted that not until 1917 did the "institutional framework of the established governments" break under pressure.

The only avenue open is forward. There is overwhelming evidence that hereafter foreign policy is going to be developed with the full participation of the people; there is no other alternative. This will require an educational effort, not in the schools alone but all the time and in every walk of life, that surpasses anything known before.

The American people can learn. We had political generals when the situation was not critical, but when the first World War came Wilson resisted all pressures to let even distinguished men like Theodore Roosevelt "raise a regiment." Since then we have developed a professional military personnel of a high order of training and ability. On the whole, except when military leaders invited another course, they have been shielded from politics, and disciplined when they dabbled.

The government has learned—not perfectly, nor as fast as Utopians might wish—to use professional scientists and technologists in a thousand ways. That also belongs not to "simple" days gone by when there were no "hard decisions," such as the future of slavery; it is part of the history of mass democracy.

The government has found how to employ economists, fiscal experts, and many others in fighting inflation, in hedging against depression, and in the management of the vast debt. That was never done before the era of mass democracy. Indeed, a review of the five years after the close of the second World War suggests that the public had, on the whole, a more accurate realization of the dangers of inflation than public officers; people curbed their buying, saved upon a scale never before known, and balanced their budgets before the government dared to do so.

Democratic diplomacy is here; it is here to stay. As in military, scientific, and fiscal matters, the nation can and will use professional diplomatists. It will master the problem more easily if there is no attempt at nostalgic escapes into the past, and no search for models abroad which do not fit our needs.

☆

☆

☆

☆

book II

PUBLIC OPINION

AND DIPLOMACY

☆

☆

☆

☆

6

The American Temper

Never before in history, at no other place in the world, has a government of continental size, actively controlled by public opinion, faced issues either in scale and scope or in difficulty and complexity such as now confront the United States. This is the fundamental frame of reference in which all discussion of democratic diplomacy must take place, else the discussion becomes irrelevant and misleading.

The United States is one nation, but its climate has every variation from the arctic to the tropic. Within its boundaries are vast differences in the soil and the many crops each produces. Beneath the earth are great numbers of minerals and metals. Consequently there are enormous ranges of occupations and preoccupations. Population pressures vary from the density of Rhode Island to the sparseness of Nevada. Its people include racial stocks from every continent, and practically every country on the globe. Despite all these and many other diverse elements, it is the only nation of continental size without regional nationalisms like the Welsh or Scots in Great Britain, or the Uzbecs and Georgians in the Soviet Union. Never before have so many people of such an infinite number of origins made one nation, with one speech and one culture.

To appreciate the unique character of the United States we must take our cue from a statement of the Spanish philosopher, Ortega y Gasset: "We have need of history in its entirety." Short-term and partial outlooks defeat every effort at comprehension. This nation illustrates his further remark that the purpose of such complete understanding of history is "not to fall back into it, but to see if we can escape from it." That our forefathers sought to escape is manifest in our revolutionary origins. John Adams was proud to have put in the Constitution of Massachusetts "a government of laws, not of men"; he regarded that as a new concept. The drafters of the Constitution for our Federal government eschewed any supreme legislature like the British Parliament; they believed in checks and balances. The Bill of Rights had to be incorporated into the Constitution to make its framework acceptable to popular sentiment.

The egalitarian philosophy, apparent from the very beginning in the Declaration of Independence, grew in scope and intensity and brought universal suffrage. The nation came in the fullness of time to emphasize its democracy more than its representative character. Through all trials and dangers faith in freedom—political, social, religious, economic—remained central. The concept of freedom itself expanded and became more and more nearly all-inclusive.

When we reflect upon our situation in this frame of reference, it is obvious that the current American attitude about the total world position of the United States in all its relationships must inevitably be exceedingly complex. Any stereotyped description, therefore, cannot furnish even an approximation of democratic public opinion regarding international questions. Nothing is more common, or less useful, than vague generalizations on the matter. Words such as "isolationist" and "internationalist" are often employed without any clear indication of their meaning in specific instances. Every effort to fix that kind of plain label on policy is certain to involve misbranding, for mere slogans cannot epitomize such intricate patterns of thought and action.

This should not be surprising; we are familiar enough with the fact that an individual's attitudes are not only complex, but that different sectors of the same person's views are frequently out of harmony, sometimes, indeed, at war with one another. A people who give so much attention to psychiatry and keep so many psychiatrists busy should have little difficulty in comprehending that fact.

Moreover, in the matters with which we are concerned there is no "man in the street"; he is as much a myth as the "economic man" with whom our fathers concerned themselves to their infinite confusion. Likewise, there is no such thing as an "average opinion," and the thoughts of no one can be called those of the "Average American." It has been fashionable to gather data about various "averages," for example the "average IQ" of our soldiers, which is said to be at "about the twelve-year-old level." Actually there is no twelve-year-old level, and averages mean nothing. But the discussion has led many to feel that we are a nation, if not of morons, at least with moronic tendencies. Surveys have been relied upon to "prove" that students "don't know any American history," and polls satisfy some observers that very few people have clear or sound knowledge or opinion about public issues.

It has become fashionable to publicize all these statistical constructs and comment upon them in extravagant terms. The needs of primary and secondary education are discussed under such startling titles as *Our Children Are Cheated*. We are told how many classrooms we are "short," how many teachers are "substandard." We are buried in statistics whose meaning is vitiated because the "standards" by which our deficiencies are measured have never existed anywhere, at any time, under the assumptions upon which we work, and with the objective of schooling for all for as long a time as they can profit by it.

Thus we are led to discount unduly the most massive achievement in popular education which the world has ever seen. Like all human endeavors, our schools have deficiencies, even some serious ones. But the technique of denouncing all that has been done as "failure" gives no incentive for improvement. Success breeds confidence; failure breeds discouragement. We ought to remember that when looking at all our tasks. If there is a sense of achievement behind us, we can press on to new and more difficult attainments. That our educational system has been fundamentally sound is evidenced by the adaptability, resourcefulness, imagination, and skill that made it possible for a people civilian in thought and habit to mobilize their energies to win victories in two successive wars over nations steeped in militarism. What country, anywhere, met the "realities" any better, whether those realities are defined as political, social, economic, or military?

Substantively we are the most literate great nation in the world, with museums, theaters, orchestras, libraries to an extent unmatched. The means for the cultivation of intelligence through higher education are available—and used— to a degree never before dreamed of. Larger and larger percentages of those with interest and talent for college work are in attendance, and they come from every social and economic "level." There are weaknesses, of course; some are genuine and some are made to look more terrifying than they should by statistical juggling. Certainly our deficiencies are serious enough to prevent smugness, but they are not acute enough to provoke despair.

If we assume ignorance, disinterest, and incompetence when discussing public opinion about foreign affairs, we arrive at a dim outlook upon democracy in general and our governmental procedures in particular. Under such circumstances the results of attempts to summarize "the American attitude," always quite imprecise, become completely misleading. One such sweeping assertion is that public opinion has been "disastrously wrong" on most great issues.

"American public opinion," like popular sentiment in any great nation, must be the composite of the views of large numbers of people, some well-informed, some with vague ideas, and some almost totally ignorant. If all this wisdom and ignorance are to be embodied in a single amalgam, every variation in the proportion of knowledge to naïvete will bring divergent opinions, and variations in the estimates of that proportion will cause different people to reach different conclusions about the character and the validity of public opinion.

Not only do individuals vary; so also do geographic areas. Regions within the United States tend to develop characteristic patterns of opinion. Because circumstances governing opinion are not uniform, very different judgments may well be wholly valid in different places in so vast a nation. Even within specific areas numberless factors are considered from many different, yet legitimate, points of view.

Complexity is heightened not only by the varying localities where opinions are formed but by differing geographical and national outlooks. Indeed, a single individual may take an isolationist view of our relations with Europe, a cooperative position regarding Central and South America, and believe in an activist policy in the Far East. Aggregates of opinion may be broken down almost indefinitely; the same person, for example, may be bitterly anti-imperialist where the colonies of certain nations are concerned and either blind to colonialism or tolerant of it in the case of other powers. If all the permutations and combinations are taken into account, the opportunities for personal "inconsistencies" are literally limitless. When all these individual variabilities are added together, the inadequacy of the simple labels so widely used is made starkly clear.

These things being so, "the American attitude" should be defined as that part of public opinion which, on a given issue, becomes articulate, and which is held with enough conviction and tenacity to affect public policy. It is not determined by counting noses, or by taking polls. It is not always, therefore, the "will of the majority," numerically determined; it may be the will of a relatively small but vocal and influential minority. On successive issues this effectively dominant group will vary enormously in its size and its make-up. The "intellectuals" may have influence at one moment, "business" at another, labor at still another; racial minorities may affect policy positively, as toward Ireland and Israel—or negatively, as in relation to Oriental immigration.

No matter what the "attitude of the people" may be, it is not the attitude of every individual even in the group dominant over the matter in hand. Many in the total would have preferred a policy differing in some—maybe a very large—degree; they joined in getting the available possibility most nearly matching their own desires and judgments. Always, moreover, there will be a "minority"; in numbers it may far exceed the "majority," but still be ineffective because its views are scattered over such a wide spectrum of opinion as not to be identifiable, or at least not persuasive.

This is dramatized by the position of the "independent" voter. The candidate in no party is acceptable to him in all the promised policies, but the citizen has no alternative but to cast his ballot for the one who offends his own beliefs the least. It is not the independent voter alone who has to grapple with this dilemma. Even among the party faithful are large groups who would have preferred some other candidate, with some other attitudes and policies. The chosen candidate is usually accepted with a wry grimace, but sometimes, as in the last two elections, considerable numbers "bolt." They do not vote in favor of the other party so much as they vote against their own in the hope of cutting down the faction in their party which "put over" a distasteful choice.

When, therefore, it is suggested as a means of improving American foreign policy that the people should choose the President and give him power virtually unchecked, it is no solution at all to the problem of foreign relations. On what basis would he act if chosen? It is notorious that men in power do not follow the line their supporters were led to expect. Franklin Roosevelt's first election was on promises of economy in government, shrinking the overgrown bureaucracy, saving our way into prosperity. He reversed his policy and was reelected on a program of spending our way into prosperity. Not all who voted for him on one platform voted for him on the other, but the "effective majority" followed his lead.

This is a sharp reminder that "the American attitude" has not remained a fixed quantity over the years on policies domestic or international. Historically it has varied enormously, partly by reason of the changed position of the United States, and partly because of the relative precision or the factor of error in successive contemporary estimates of our situation. For attitudes are shaped not merely by the facts, but by what are supposed to be the facts; in many instances those are two quite different aggregates.

In making any estimate one must be acutely aware of all these—and many other—variables, and also of the subjective nature of every expression of opinion. Yet if we are to form a judgment upon a question of vital public concern, it is essential to express a view. With these qualifications in mind, it seems to me that at the moment the dominant mood regarding the position of the United States in the world is a compound of assurance, at one fringe of our society amounting to arrogance, and of doubt, in some instances alarmingly close to defeatism. Many of the same people who assert that the United States is the greatest nation in the world show the most fear of the Soviets—of their capacity to infiltrate our institutions of government and enterprise, of their power to outstrip us in weapons and in diplomacy. They remind one of that passage in Ortega y Gasset wherein he said our epoch is "superior to other times, [but] inferior to itself"; "strong, indeed, and at the same time uncertain of its destiny; proud of its strength and at the same time fearing it."

In this we have not been able to "escape from" history. Thirty-four years ago, in 1922, it was said, "The storm is just ended, and we are as anxious and disturbed as though it were about to break. . . . We have vague hopes, precise fears. Our fears are infinitely more precise than our hopes. . . . Demoralization and doubt are in us and with us." That generation was described as unhappy, living among great events "whose echoes will fill our entire life." The worst casualty was "the mind. The mind has indeed been cruelly wounded. . . . It passes a mournful judgment on itself. It doubts itself profoundly."

Such an atmosphere smoothed the way for the totalitarians. Ortega y Gasset expressed it with great clarity: "Many men . . . homesick for the herd . . . devote themselves passionately to whatever is left in them of the sheep. They want to march through life together, along the collective path, shoulder to shoulder, wool rubbing wool, and the head down."

At the outbreak of the second World War, a well-known American author wrote: "This war . . . is but a symptom of a revolution. . . . This . . . will mean the liquidation of the modern state, of modern society, after three brief centuries of splendor. More deeply, it will mean the liquidation of the basic human value, of the ruling sense of man's meaning to himself as an individual within the mystery of life, which has subsumed and shaped the modern era." A philosopher compressed the idea into two words, "intellectual panic."

At the recent Bandung Conference President Soekarno of Indonesia made it clear that he thought the same negative forces are powerfully at work in our own times. "We are living," he said, "in a world of fear . . . fear of the future, fear of the hydrogen bomb, fear of ideologies. Perhaps this fear is a greater danger than the danger itself, because it is fear which drives men to act foolishly, to act thoughtlessly, to act dangerously."

One could wish that it might honestly be said that the United States had escaped any infection from these viruses which have poisoned the lives of one nation after another. That is too much to expect. This much is true: the United States escaped the worst of the modern political infections. But the discouragement of many intellectuals and leading commentators with democracy and its characteristic processes is one manifestation of the fact that we were not unscathed. The furor over "security" and the shrieking headlines about investigations were other evidences.

In a notable speech before the United Nations General Assembly in October 1946, Molotov, the Soviet Foreign Minister, openly taunted the United States for its loss of self-confidence, the waning of our belief that the future belongs to our type of democracy. Clearly referring to the United States he said: "There is no lack of faith among our [Soviet] people in the peaceful means of progress and there is no feeling of incertitude which is created in countries with unstable economic and political prospects." He went on to speak of America's "profound distrust in the peaceful methods of further development of one's own country and of some pessimistic lack of confidence in one's own strength in so far as the prospect of peaceful competition between states and social systems is concerned."

Fortunately that mood is passing. The avoidance of the postwar depression, predicted not only by Soviet propagandists but by many "experts" at home, did much to restore faith in an economy which was repeatedly called unstable, yet proved strong enough to rescue Western Europe from economic collapse. Renewed confidence was stimulated by our ability to rearm, fight a bitter struggle in Korea, and establish alliances to check the Soviets without any of the predicted Furies—fatal inflation, drastic depression, or crippling taxes.

There is urgent need further to recover faith in our own institutions. They are far from perfect, but they are indigenous; they have served us well in meeting earlier crises; they have shown unusual capacity for adaptation to meet new circumstances, and will continue to change with time. We have every reason to renew our faith that the ideals and principles upon which they are founded are, indeed, the last, best hope of mankind.

It is unnecessary to resort to nostalgia in order to recover faith in the future of the United States. Indeed we cannot, as Ortega y Gasset said, "fall back into" history. The founding fathers were but men like ourselves, with faults as well as outstanding virtues. There was plenty of dirty politics in the early days of the Republic. Even then men sometimes were close to despair; Jefferson said we were tending rapidly toward monarchy; he was as wrong in that estimate as he was right in many another. If all the politicians of bygone days had been statesmen, there would have been no Civil War. If Lincoln's Second Inaugural had remained the keynote of the Reconstruction Era, there would be no Solid South with a one-party system. Clearly we cannot turn back nor, if we read "history in its entirety," would we want to, for the record is a mixture of greatness and of sordid episodes. But we can abandon what has proved wrong, and work on the premises which have stood the test of time and have become firmer in the trials to which they have been subjected.

7

American Policy

In the United States foreign policy is the expression of the will of the people. Even the daily operations of international action are affected by public opinion, but by no means so profoundly as its basic postulates. Nevertheless, if a President or Secretary of State seems too belligerent or too passive, or functions in any way that really irritates the public, he is under great pressure to alter his tactics or, if he is a Secretary of State, to resign.

What do we mean by "policy" and "tactics"? Currently the word "policy" has been almost destroyed by over-use. It should not be employed to describe every diplomatic decision, every tactical move in international affairs. When that is done great confusion ensues; the over-use of the word "policy" has had that effect in a marked degree recently.

Perhaps an illustration will highlight the difference between policy as basic objective and tactics as a means to an end. When one is sailing, it is sometimes necessary to tack because a boat cannot sail right up into the wind. From the window beside which I write in the summer I can see as many as twenty small sailboats racing. All have to start at the same line, round the same buoys, and finish at the starting point. That defines their objective; in foreign affairs that is "policy." But at any given moment, depending upon their tactical approach, the different boats are tacking in opposite directions; a person who never saw a regatta before would insist that they could not be racing against one another; he would be confused by the variety of tactical maneuvers employed in seeking the same goal. He would be even more surprised to know that two boats which pursued opposite tactics finished in virtually a dead heat.

The word "policy," then, should be reserved for fundamental objectives. In general, these are stable; they alter relatively slowly, though dramatic episodes may make long-developing changes seem sudden. The ebb and flow of daily circumstances over these underlying realities occasion many tactical maneuvers, which do not involve new policy. It is about the day-to-day changes of pace, or of temporary direction "while on the wrong tack," that most public discussion rages; the argument is over the tactics of the moment rather than the fixed national objectives.

The Monroe Doctrine is a first-class illustration of basic policy. Its roots go back to the days of Washington. The elements of which it was constructed appeared in a number of different episodes. In 1823 what had been evolving was summarized and stated in a brief, clear, and explicit way under dramatic circumstances. This crystallized "policy" into "doctrine." Sometimes it is asserted that the Monroe Doctrine could not be a basic objective because it has not been uniformly "enforced." That word represents a serious misconception. The Doctrine was not a law, not a fiat, but a desideratum. Occasionally there was no opportunity to act effectively, as for example when Maximilian set up his Empire in Mexico while we were fully occupied with the Civil War. The same situation existed during the brief Spanish "annexation" of Santo Domingo. At other times those in charge lacked the understanding, the energy, the skill, or even the will to pursue our fundamental national objectives. None of these circumstances affected either the reality or the validity of the policy itself.

The inclusion of Canada within our defensive perimeter is another policy; it is as old as the Rush-Bagot agreement of 1817. As soon as our northern border became virtually "open," that is undefended, we had to see to it that Canada could not be employed as a base of operations against us. When President Franklin Roosevelt made the policy perfectly explicit he was merely stating formally what had long been implicit.

Isolation was long a basic policy of the United States, as we saw in Book I. It was clearly foreshadowed in the neutrality decision of 1793, and appeared in almost classic fashion in Washington's Farewell Address. "Isolation" illustrates a fact which is often overlooked: policy is not absolute dogma; there is always a relative quality about it. So there were always important qualifications to our isolationist concept. There was nothing isolationist about Commodore Perry's trip to Japan; in 1853 he summed up his viewpoint: "The tide of empire is gradually flowing westward. . . .

From the geographical position of the United States, and their rapidly growing commerce between the shores of the Pacific and China, and the Polynesian Islands, our people must naturally be drawn into the contest for empire."

One cannot follow contemporary discussion of our national interest without seeing that isolation had more relevance with reference to Europe than to Asia. That was natural enough; it was from Europe we had won independence. The great powers that might menace us were all European. Asia, on the other hand, was a political vacuum. Naturally, therefore, policy toward Asia did not rest on all fours with policy relating to Europe.

But isolation was sometimes modified even with reference to Europe. We always had a deep concern in the freedom of the seas. The peace-loving Jefferson took our infant navy out of mothballs to fight the Barbary pirates in the war with Tripoli. American squadrons visited the eastern Mediterranean long ago, and the United States had a lively interest in the question of the Dardanelles before we were a great power, or held primacy on the sea. Our nation took the lead in putting an end to the Danish "Sound dues"; we insisted that Skagerrak and Kattegat be opened during the Buchanan administration, usually regarded as feeble.

We tend to forget—perhaps some of us do not even know —that for many years the very existence of the United States was regarded—and rightly—as a threat to the stability of thrones and the integrity of empires. Three basic factors explain our expansionist character which underlaid Europe's fears concerning the United States.

The first was our revolutionary origin. Our struggle for independence belongs so far back in the dim past that we are apt to take it for granted, and fail to appreciate to the full its dynamic character. Revolutions do not make a full turn and then stop; they develop momentum. Those who wished separation from Britain, and no more, were certain, therefore, to be disappointed. The phrases of the Declaration of Independence promised much more than simple divorce, and the longer the war lasted the more drastic would be the changes. With all the continuities carried over from centuries of British constitutional development, the American Revolution nonetheless produced a very sharp break from the past. There were ideological elements that seemed to Europeans exceedingly menacing. The French Revolution, which was influenced markedly by the American, appeared to many on the Continent and in Britain to demonstrate the validity of such fears.

Abraham Lincoln said that our Declaration of Independence "gave liberty not alone to the people of this country, but hope to all the world, for all future time." The great seal of the United States carries in Latin the motto, a new order of the world; that is proof positive that we deliberately sought a break with the past and expected our order to extend to other parts—all parts—of the world. Such sentiments, often repeated, have worn a smooth path through our minds. They slip from our lips without clear realization of the dimensions of what they actually promised, but those who do not fully share our ideology are acutely conscious of their revolutionary implications even now.

The second expansive, indeed explosive, force was encouraged by a virtually empty continent. Restless and adventurous men and women, such as had settled in the wilderness between the Atlantic and the mountains, and had engaged in revolution, would not be content to remain out of the promised land to the west. The occupation of the present area of the United States involved a dynamic that makes other movements of population pale by comparison.

It was inevitable that, when the shores of the Pacific were reached, some mastery of that mighty ocean would seem essential. As we have seen, Commodore Perry predicted that we would advance to the shores of Asia. William H. Seward was the most explicit political exponent of further expansion. He said that Russia was building on the Arctic Ocean the outpost of the United States; he purchased Alaska. He inherited the desire for Canada, which the "war-hawks" at the time of the War of 1812 had hoped to capture. The idea that Canada should remain independent of the United States died hard; remnants of annexationist sentiment survived into the twentieth century. Seward also expected the addition of Mexico and foresaw Mexico City as "the ultimate central seat of the power of the North American people." The predictions of Seward can now be too easily written off as extravagant; they accurately reflected the expansionist temper of a large segment of the American people in the nineteenth century.

The third expansionist element was our traditional advocacy of democracy. The strength of this factor, like the others, is now underestimated. We think of communism as the really expansionist force. There is no longer any doubt that the whole Communist dogma is built upon the assumption that its doctrine will spread to all the world. This idea is so integrally woven into party and official thought and action that it may fairly be said to occupy a key position in the structure of Soviet long-range policy. Any deviation from it, therefore, may safely be assumed to be tactical— a momentary halt while attempting to regroup for some new advance. Even when the top men are all smiles, and honey takes the place of vitriol in the Soviet press, the substance of that particular policy remains reasonably constant. Any time the Soviet leaders lose confidence that they are riding the wave of the future their whole ideological foundation will be destroyed.

In our concentration upon Soviet aggression we are likely to overlook the fact that democracy, also, has been expansive, and in its American manifestation at least, inherently so. We developed a recognition policy which equated *de facto* with *de jure*; it was designed to facilitate revolutions such as that which had won our freedom. We sought to propagate democratic institutions in Latin America; we watched the "liberal" efforts at revolution in Europe in 1848 with earnest hopefulness. The eagerness of our government to recognize Kossuth, the Hungarian revolutionist, brought a protest from the Austrian Chargé Hülsemann. Daniel Webster responded with an eloquence which breathed the spirit of confidence in our future; he made the point that, without attempting intervention, we were deeply concerned with "the fortunes of nations struggling for institutions like our own." We never acquiesced in tyranny, we never accepted absolutism or statism. We always protested them. John Quincy Adams recorded with satisfaction his lecture to the Russian Minister, Baron Tuyll, on the virtues of republican government and our determination to "contest the right of Russia to any territorial establishment on this continent."

The tradition found its ultimate expression when Woodrow Wilson made his declaration, "The world must be made safe for democracy." That prophecy is not often quoted in America these days, though once it was on every tongue. But it has not been forgotten elsewhere. Others appreciate more than we now do that it was predicated upon the firm belief that the world could not always—or even long—endure half democratic and half tyrannous. His aphorism was founded upon the assumption that safety for democracy could be attained only in a world where democratic ideals and democratic institutions became, if not absolutely universal, at least dominant.

President Eisenhower made the same point with a characteristically different emphasis: "The great struggle of our times is for . . . the hearts and souls of men—their very inmost souls. If we are going to be strong we must be strong in spirit." "We must be devoted with all our heart to the values we defend. We must know that each of these values and virtues applies with equal force at the ends of the earth and in our relations with our neighbors next door." "We must reaffirm to the oppressed masses of the earth the great truth that the God who gave life to humanity, at the same time gave the right to liberty to man." Our principles, he reasserted upon another occasion, "do not permit our acquiescing in the perpetual enslavement of any peoples."

Seen in long perspective, it is indubitable, therefore, that both communism and democracy involve conscious, indeed determined, breaks with the past. Each must believe in its own future and tie its hopes of security to the acceptance by others of its political, social, and economic philosophy. Neither has been content to be an island in a hostile sea; each has been expansionist in spirit. They have that in common; the contrast is in method and objective; democracy is dedicated to freedom, communism to control through domination.

In the United States all these historical elements united with other aspects of the national interest to prevail over traditional isolation when the crises of world war arose in this century. The tradition of our New Order in the World proved stronger than the hope we could steer clear of European involvements. When we had grown to the stature of a great power, it was inevitable that we should find it a fundamental interest not supinely to permit any aggressor nation to control the whole continent of Europe—or, for that matter, Asia. This made our participation in both world wars of the twentieth century absolutely inevitable. Whatever the confusions at moments of decision, the perspective of history makes that clear.

There is now a general consensus that we are caught up in the great tide of world events. Some feel we are being carried along by the swiftness and strength of the current in directions we cannot control. Others assert that we are in a masterful position and can direct the course of history, determining the channel through which events shall flow. There is general agreement that we are in the world, and must play a great, if not a decisive, role. This is a tremendous gain, for it means that there is no such studied attempt to retreat from reality as occurred after the first World War. No one in a place of effective leadership has recently spoken of "normalcy" as though it were possible to undo, or at least forget, a part of history that was dramatically costly in life and treasure; all recognize that recent events are certain to affect profoundly our social structure and economic customs in ways that will not be statistically evident for a generation or more.

8

Experience as Teacher

Despite the consensus that we have a great role to play in shaping the course of world history, there is a strong current of pessimism regarding our capacity to act wisely in meeting so great a responsibility. It is asserted that public opinion has been "disastrously wrong" in moments of great decision. Instability, swift changes of mood, emotionalism, lurching from one extreme to the other are commonly charged against the American democracy. The alleged weakness of the executive as compared with the legislative is another ground for doubt of our ability adequately to meet the challenge of the times.

Perhaps we should not be surprised at such critical attitudes; it may be a natural reaction from earlier exuberance. Few now upon the world stage experienced the era of overconfidence of which Woodrow Wilson became the acknowledged spokesman. His eloquence was that of a recent convert; it is not unusual to find the newly convinced speaking with deepest passion. His later utterances which are now remembered were a far cry from his request at the outbreak of war in Europe that the American people remain "neutral in fact as well as in name. . . . impartial in thought as well as in action." The phrases which made him a world figure were potent war-cries rather than wise guides toward peace. The slogan "a war to end war" was clearly a poor program for achieving peace; it obscured the essentially political nature of peace; it made victory and peace appear synonymous. "Open covenants . . . openly arrived at" suggested a "new diplomacy" which contrasted with old methods. Yet when Wilson came to act in the Paris negotiations the phrase rose to haunt him, for it proved impossible of fulfillment; he found secrecy essential to negotiation.

From such exalted dreams, there was a sharp reaction to a fictitious "normalcy" and a blindly unrealistic "they hired the money" attitude toward interallied debts. A censorious mood is inevitable for any commentator who fastens his attention upon such swift changes of temper and action and who feels that as a consequence the peace was needlessly lost. Certainly no one could assert that wise courses were consistently followed. Indeed, it is not too much to say that the follies of that era led directly to the great depression, paved the way for Fascism and Nazism, and thus contributed fuel for the second World War.

Let us concede that point; even so, the case against de-

mocracy and its allegedly weak leadership would still not
be proved. What evidence is there that if Germany had won
the first World War the Kaiser and his clique would have
chosen a wiser course? Everything we know of their aims,
ideals, and methods makes it clear that the world would
have been worse off if Germany had been the victor. When
Russia was under the coherent dominance of Stalin, and
Italy was ready to leave all decisions to Il Duce, and Hitler
was master of Germany, did the strength of these leaders
cause them to walk in paths of sane and sober statesmanship
toward peace? Let us admit that many of our actions and
attitudes were shortsighted; let us go further and concede
that too often there was a flight from responsibility and
sometimes even from reality. But was our nation ever involved in anything so dastardly as Stalin's pact with Hitler,
and his participation in the rape of Poland?

For the moment it is unnecessary to insist upon the virtues
of democracy; it is enough to appeal to a cold comparison
with the other available forms of government and their
characteristic historical behavior. If there is no reason to
be proud of some of our sins of omission, we need not feel
the blush of shame for gross sins of commission such as those
of Mussolini, Hitler, Stalin, or the military clique of Japan.
"Strong leaderhip," relatively free from the "whims" of
public sentiment, is no program for peace through wisdom;
it often substitutes the irrational, even quixotic, impulses of
a Duce, a Fuehrer, a Stalin. The recent repudiation of
Stalinism—the strength of steel—by the new leaders of the
Kremlin completes the cycle. He was the last of the "strong"
men to be renounced by his successors. It is striking that
there has been no like repudiation of the democratic leaders
of our time. There have, indeed, been criticisms; their errors
of judgment have been described and sometimes denounced,

but they are not reviled and held up to scorn.

Acid commentators on our national "failures" often forget the simplest of all truths—it takes many to make or keep the peace; it requires only one reckless leader in a post of power to start a war. No one who knows his ABC's would contend that in the twentieth century any democracy wanted or sought war. On the other hand, as soon as Ribbentrop made his cynical deal with Molotov, it was clear to neutral statesmen in Norway, for example, that it was a war pact. Hitler and Stalin were not caught in a tide and carried into war against their will; they designed war. When it came, the war did not follow their design, but that they intended war is indubitable. In the same way, it has been revealed that Japanese militarists took a leaf from Bismarck's book; as he made the Ems dispatch intentionally misleading, so they deliberately changed the sense of an American note in order to precipitate war.

The preamble of UNESCO says that "wars begin in the minds of men." That is a large generalization. It is obvious upon a moment's thought that war can begin in the mind in two entirely separate ways—by design and by error. It can be argued that democratic statesmen miscalculated the forces at work, and misread the signs of the times to such a degree as to make war more likely or, to put the case as strongly as anyone could wish, to make war inevitable. The other way in which wars begin in the minds of men is by deliberate intent; to describe that situation it would have been more precise to say that they originate in the hearts of men. The mind of democracy may not have been so clear and perceptive as it needed to be, but its heart did not harbor lust for war. Neither World War was conceived in democracy; both were precipitated by violently antidemocratic regimes under strong leadership.

Nor is our structure of government responsible for the delay in reading aright the signs of the times. There are critics who assert that the division of powers fixed by our Constitution makes policy incoherent, that the President has no such control as the Prime Minister of Britain. But who would want to exchange our errors for the bumbling of Baldwin's government or Neville Chamberlain's proclamation of "peace in our time" after capitulating to Hitler? Save for the phenomenon of Briand's personal strength, who would choose the kaleidoscopic government of France in exchange for ours? Who would seriously propose that the checks and balances which did not exist for Mussolini or Hitler or Stalin should be dropped from the structure of our government? No one wants such "strong" leadership as to make us subject to like powers of personal decision.

The hard and inescapable fact is that, though man is perfectible, most of us are not perfect. It is, therefore, folly to appeal to later experience in order to flagellate ourselves for lack of foresight. One prominent writer, a sharp critic of American foreign policy, does just that in an extraordinary sentence: "Now that the book is done, I am much better aware than I was before writing it how wide has been the gap between my own insight and my own hindsight." He goes further and confesses: "I am criticising others for holding views which at the time I may myself have shared, or for a lack of foresight of which I was also guilty." Nearly every public figure of Germany or Japan who helped to precipitate war could have written those sentences if he had any residue of conscience. Surely they furnish no basis for an indictment of the democratic process of policy formation, or for the results of democratic action or inaction.

It is possible to go much further. The author of those words has spent his whole adult life as student, participator, and commentator on international affairs. He could qualify in any court as an expert. If the gap between his insight and hindsight proved so wide, from whom could we expect such leadership that the gap would disappear? The argument carries within itself its own refutation. It is not lack of strength that leads to error; it is deficiency in knowledge, wisdom, insight. If no one and no group could master the facts which constituted reality, if no one and no group made a correct estimate of the situation, including the "strong" leaders of whom the earth has had a plenty in the first half of the twentieth century, how can this be made the basis for the indictment of democracy and of the structure of our government?

Much of this recent criticism arises from the fact that the critics take far too egocentric a view. The world has inherited a set of irresistible forces bequeathed to this generation by those very statesmen who, we are told with rare historical inaccuracy, were not faced with "hard decisions." They made easy decisions to grab territories, to create empires, to be niggardly in preparing "nations" for self-rule. "The White Man's burden" was a phrase with an overtone of contempt, as well as the substance of arrogance.

The colonizing nations exported Western products and Western ideas into the East. Some of the products and some of the practices were not good for the people; some were inappropriate; others were valuable. Those which were not good for the natives laid the basis, all too often, though not always justifiably, for the charge that Western nations were guilty of exploitation. Exploitation was not the worst sin; the disastrous error was the pride which goeth before destruction. The failure to be more appreciatively sensitive to Eastern cultures is epitomized in Kipling's other well-remembered phrase: "East is East, and West is West, and never the twain shall meet." The assumption of superiority by the West led to deep resentments which remain now that the substance of imperialism is virtually at an end. Some of the resentments inculcated in the Asians they are repaying with a vengeance.

Decisions, not hard enough, taken long ago by those diplomatists whose passing is now so regretted by commentators dubious of democracy, sowed the wind. We are now reaping the whirlwind. Those of us who live on the shores of Cape Cod know that when a hurricane hits there is nothing one can do about it; there are some things one can do about his property—stow it away and batten it down—and some things one can do about himself—seek shelter on high ground. It was a Socialist government of Britain that measured the velocity of the rising winds of nationalism and retreated just in time from India, Pakistan, Burma. An American government of mass democracy, whose "institutional framework" was said to have "broken" under popular pressure, advanced the date of Philippine independence, and avoided tragedy there.

The plain fact is there are no pat "solutions" available for some situations. The French have a problem in North Africa; it was long in building; it is complex in structure and intractable in substance. No one who has read history would expect even those now-lauded elegant Ministers-of-State, who were not dominated by the masses, but who laid the foundations of the current crisis, to find smooth, easy, and permanent cures today. It is no shame upon their successors that they cannot either. The mixture of Jew, Moslem, and Christian in the Levant has made for tension since before the Crusades. The addition of oil, wealth, poverty, imperialism, aggression, subversion, fanatic nationalism to earlier ingredients makes an explosive combination. No classic diplomatist serving an irresponsible executive could readily resolve the troubles brewing for more than a thousand years. Failure to package a neat, clear, effective antidote to all the poisons is no ground for criticizing democratic diplomacy. This is especially true when the greatest antidemocratic nation in the world is determined to make trouble, and prevent peace.

The argument might rest at this point with the assertion that our democracy is no worse than other forms of government in policy formation or action because of divided powers. As an exercise in negative proof it would be adequate, though no one could feel very happy about it. There is a positive side of the argument, however, which deserves thoughtful attention.

So far as the United States is concerned, the second World War, like the first, was fought under the leadership of a President who could fairly be called an isolationist when he took office. Though Franklin Roosevelt as candidate for Vice President in the Cox campaign had enthusiastically supported the League of Nations, he abandoned the League during his presidential campaign. References to foreign affairs in his inaugural address, save for the "good neighbor" policy toward Latin America, had a strongly isolationist cast. International trade, he said, is, "in point of time and necessity, secondary to the establishment of a sound national economy. I favor as a practical policy the putting of first things first."

Not long after Roosevelt took office he torpedoed the International Economic Conference in London because of complete misapprehension of the economic relationship of the United States to the rest of the world. As Wilson had been preoccupied with the "new freedom" at home, so Roosevelt was absorbed in a "new deal" in domestic affairs and did not realize how closely interacting were those things we call, for convenience, "foreign" and those we call "domestic." Neither President, when his administration opened, looked abroad with clear vision or perceptive insight.

Subsequent events helped to clarify Roosevelt's thinking. Nevertheless, despite broad general statements favoring closer international relations, many of his acts sought to limit American commitments as much as possible. For example, though he spoke of "allies," he entered upon no treaties of alliance. Cooperation was governed by executive agreements, never submitted to the Senate or to Congress for approval. Like Wilson, however, he came to see that we had lost our isolated position, not as a matter of will but through the sheer operation of events in the fields of transportation, communication, science, technology, industrial production, commercial development, and a whole host of other historical realities.

In particular, the essentiality of the survival of Britain for the security of the United States became evident, even if it were not worth saving for its contributions to political thought and action. The President, therefore, made the exchange of destroyers for bases, initiated lend-lease, espoused the idea of the United Nations.

It is unnecessary to make any estimate as to whether, in this transition, Mr. Roosevelt led public opinion or followed it; for present purposes any such exactitude in attempting to measure the incommensurate is not important. It suffices to say that none of the principal acts or major foreign policies by which the revolution in his thought and action was symbolized would have been possible without public support which was general enough to be ungoverned by partisanship—though partisanship was always present on both sides, and often dominant in other matters. Indeed, some of the measures raised Constitutional questions which would have created grave difficulties but for the strong backing of public opinion.

Moreover, the United States has not retreated from that bipartisan conversion from isolationist dreams to an active role in world affairs. In the face of such massive proof that our democracy does learn from experience, we can forgive some costly errors arising from lack of foresight. We now know that demobilization was too swift and went too far directly following the war. As early as November 1944 Roosevelt told Churchill that immediately after Germany's collapse he would "bring American troops home as rapidly as transportation problems will permit."

The final decision was taken by President Truman; it was the act of a strong executive, for it was ordered by the President in his capacity as commander-in-chief, in which phase of his powers the executive is subject to the least control. It was taken at a moment when there was a minimum of restraint upon his action. There is no question that he had the support of public opinion, but in this instance general approval was to some extent, at least, a secondary result of wartime security measures, which kept the people from knowing the deficiencies in the wartime alliance and the menace of Soviet expansionism.

Our rapid return to civilian rhythm was fully justified so far as our wartime enemies were concerned. Censorship had withheld, for war purposes, most of the evidence that tensions were so great within the alliance that one of our partners was likely to become a new, and bitter, enemy. Uneasy stirrings of doubt lest that should be the case were quieted when President Roosevelt, in his fireside chat on Christmas Eve, 1943, said: "The Teheran Conference . . . gave me my first opportunity to meet . . . Marshal Stalin.

We had planned to talk to each other across the table . . . but we soon found we were all on the same side of the table. We came to the Conference with faith in each other. . . . Now we have supplemented faith with definite knowledge." Again, on March 8, 1944, he said: "I think the Russians are perfectly friendly; they aren't trying to gobble up all the rest of Europe or the world. . . . They haven't got any crazy ideas of conquest . . . these fears that have been expressed by a lot of people here—with some reason—that the Russians are going to try to dominate Europe, I personally don't think there's anything in it."

That misestimate is not cited in order to criticize Mr. Roosevelt; the purpose in mentioning it is twofold. In the first place, it helps explain the way in which public opinion was misled. The President had available to him explicit reports about wartime difficulties and their plain implications which were far more reliable than the hints that leaked through censorship to the public. The experts in the Department of State were keenly aware of the intention of the Soviets to dominate Eastern Europe, and were eager to prevent it. The fact that the President had special knowledge gave his contrary opinion on such a vital matter much greater persuasiveness than would have been the case if allied tensions with Russia had been fully exposed publicly. We cannot fairly blame public opinion for failures to face up to issues unless the basic facts are available to all the people. Mr. Truman has made it clear that even as Vice President he did not have access to information which might have led him to take a view different from that of his predecessor, and so to have made a different decision regarding demobilization.

There is a second valid reason for recalling President Roosevelt's explicit reassurance regarding Soviet intentions:

it is a powerful piece of evidence that those critics are in error who feel that modern democracy goes astray in foreign policy because of the separation of powers and the need for the executive to appease the legislative. In this instance the President was virtually unchecked. His initiative in foreign affairs is always great, and waxes even greater during war and immediately thereafter. There was no appeasement of the Congress or the electorate in this deliberate judgment which could take into account much written evidence, innumerable verbal reports, and his own firsthand contacts at Cairo and Teheran.

The plain fact is that two successive Presidents, despite repeated warnings from the professional advisers, allowed the Soviets to attain a dominant position in Eastern Europe. Each step in the fatal process was clearly defined as time went on; the consequences were explained again and again. An executive, unchecked by Congress or public opinion, took the fatal decisions. They were taken at a time, moreover, when military resources and diplomatic counters could have made a different policy effective. This acquiescence in Soviet domination reflected a hope that the United States could retire from Europe after the war and assume little responsibility for what happened upon a continent where we had twice fought.

This is not an attempt to argue from the particular to the general; it is a mere illustration—one among many, but a pertinent one—of the leadership available to the President, without serious challenge arising either from partisanship or from the need to cater to Congress or to public passions. The lesson to be drawn runs counter to the thesis that strengthening the executive is the key to better policy formation; the true conclusion is that the public should have all the facts, as fully, frankly, and promptly as they can be set forth.

From a historical viewpoint, this is an astounding era in which to assert that "the power of the executive has become enfeebled, often to the verge of impotence, by the pressures of the representative assembly and of mass opinions," and that modern democracies "devitalize," "enfeeble," and "eviscerate" the executive power. When de Tocqueville wrote, his low evaluation of the Presidency was justifiable. Even when Woodrow Wilson published *Congressional Government* in 1885, there were grounds for regarding the executive as feeble. But to assert in 1954 that its power has "declined" seems bad timing indeed.

Years before that date executive leadership directed the Wilsonian reforms enacted by Congress. A little later came Franklin Roosevelt's "must" list of legislation and the extraordinary series of New Deal acts under his initiative and guidance. In 1950 it was President Truman's decision to fight in Korea—an executive act exclusively in its critical early stages. Before 1954 Congress had given support to the Truman Doctrine, to the Marshall Plan, to NATO, SEATO, and a host of precedent shattering actions, all initiated by the executive.

"Precedent shattering" is the precise term. During the first World War we had no allies; President Wilson eschewed the word as though it were poison. He spoke always of "associates," and the treaties at the end referred to the "Allied and Associated Powers." In the second World War President Roosevelt, as was noted, used the word "allies" colloquially but there were no treaties of alliance, only executive agreements. When, therefore, on April 4, 1949, we signed a treaty of alliance with eleven other nations, it was the first such engagement ever entered into after the government was organized under the Constitution. It was no less than precedent shattering when we committed ourselves to go to war by agreeing "that an armed attack against one or more . . . be considered an attack against . . . all," and promised to take "action . . . , including the use of armed force, to restore and maintain the security of the North Atlantic area." The treaty was to have a minimum duration of twenty years. Yet radical as was the break with tradition the Senate consented to ratification by the over-whelming vote of 82 to 13. It was done on the initiative of the President.

Decline in the power of the executive since the days of Rutherford B. Hayes and Chester A. Arthur, or, for that matter, Franklin Pierce and James Buchanan? That suggestion involves rewriting history with a vengeance! It was at the time when liberal democracy was only on the rise, and when the prestige of democracy was still undimmed, that the bitterest comments were uttered about the Senate as "the graveyard of treaties." John Hay who belonged to the old tradition, not the new, lamented, " 'Give and take,' the axiom of diplomacy to the rest of the world, is positively forbidden to us, by both the Senate and the public opinion. We must take what we can and give nothing, which greatly narrows our possibilities." Yet the Senate was right in calling for the renegotiation of the first Hay-Pauncefote treaty; under its goad Hay did better on the second try. Moreover, even when the Senate did not act so wisely, it was not wholly to blame. Hay sent treaties up for "advice and consent" to ratification without a word of explanation or exposition. In the light of the Constitutional powers of the Senate, this was a serious failure in cooperation by the executive.

The outstanding fact is that today the executive has the

initiative in foreign policy to a degree unknown before in our history, even in the early days of the Republic. Public demand is always for the exercise of that initiative, for clear and explicit statements of policy, for energy and adroitness in pursuit of the national objectives. There are harassments in hearings, investigations, delays. But no first-class proposal in foreign policy has been refused support since the Wilsonian debacle.

Not only has the Congress given cooperation—not blind, but very real—the public has also shown like capacity to follow executive leadership. The United Nations was launched with almost too much acclaim. The Truman Doctrine was never seriously challenged. The Marshall Plan was vigorously backed. Even the Korean war was accepted with relatively calm philosophy. It was never "popular"; why should it be? But it was necessary, and on that basis was approved by public sentiment.

9

The Marshall Plan

The Marshall Plan is a striking example of the capacity of a democracy to face reality and act in a dynamic way. Where, and by whom, it was first conceived it is unnecessary to inquire. It is not likely that it was a complete inspiration which came at one moment to a single individual. We do know that some of its outlines were exposed to public discussion before the Secretary of State brought it to the fore; the way had been prepared somewhat. When the time came it was proposed in a totally unspectacular manner; General Marshall, responding to an honorary degree at Harvard, briefly set forth the idea. He did it in such a

matter-of-fact tone and in such ordinary words, without
forensic ornamentation, that no phrases in the speech are
generally remembered or quoted.

By a stroke of genius the offered aid was made available
to nations within the Soviet orbit. "Our policy," the Secretary said, "is directed not against any country or doctrine
but against hunger, poverty, desperation, and chaos." Some
of the nations in the Soviet orbit indicated willingness to
participate and, except for a strong jerk on their leading
strings by Moscow, they would have been glad to do so. With
rare self-restraint, moreover, the suggestion was passed to
our allies; they were invited to make proposals. "It would
be neither fitting nor efficacious for this Government to
undertake to draw up unilaterally a program designed to
place Europe on its feet economically. This is the business
of the Europeans. . . . The role of this country should con-
sist of friendly aid in the drafting of a European program
and of later support of such a program so far as it may
be practical for us to do so."

The Marshall Plan, as finally operative, was a product
of allied thought. There was no American dictation, though
as the principal investor ours was a leading voice. Moreover, it was by no means an executive act alone. The proposal was not set forth with all the prestige and force of the
presidential office behind it; the initiative had been left to
the Secretary of State. To become effective, it required the
cooperation of the Congress, which was then dominated by
the party in opposition to the President. Partisanship was
acrimonious on both sides; this was the Eightieth Congress
which President Truman castigated unmercifully and continuously as a "do-nothing" Congress; the scorn heaped
upon it was rare in modern times—both in volume and bitterness.

Nevertheless, the Eightieth Congress passed the authorizations and appropriations for the Marshall Plan, heeding the Secretary's plea that "political passion and prejudice should have no part." It involved sums of money—and a consequent tax burden—that would have been not only impossible, but unimaginable, before the war—or immediately thereafter. No wonder Barbara Ward has called it "a great and creative act of statesmanship." It is the more brilliant because it was done by consensus; "the people of America" did indeed understand "the character of the problem and the remedies to be applied." Congress would never have been cooperative if public opinion had not given it a strong impulse to such action.

Critics of democratic processes will argue that the public did not, in reality, fully understand the matter. Of course, the public did not comprehend the intricacies or the multitude of details, many of which were important for the success of the Plan. Indeed, very few people ever did grasp all its complexities. To make much of that fact is to beg the question; those details are the function of experts and technicians. To argue that ignorance of such matters withdraws credit from democracy for the massive achievements which grew out of the Plan is wrong. The public may well know that a bridge should be put across a river; the community may weigh the cost in the light of expected benefits and express its conclusion in a referendum. To say that the people are not responsible because they could not design and construct the bridge is nonsense—and nonsense of a very dangerous kind.

The central facts of the matter are two. In the first place, public support of the Marshall Plan represented a fundamental economic judgment, namely that it is better to work with a prosperous competitor than an insolvent debtor. The results of that sound judgment have been nothing short of sensational; the drift toward economic ruin which gained enormous momentum during a long and costly war was reversed. Ten years after the first World War the economic collapse was upon us. The seers and the prophets, not only among the Soviets but within our own borders, were sure that we faced the same sort of collapse after the second World War.

None of the wise men who speak as though they could read the public mind suggested, and certainly none believed, that the American people would accept the level of taxation necessary to break "the vicious circle" into which the disparity between Europe's needs and capacities was driving the Continent. None of them hinted that our citizens cared that much about "restoring the confidence of the European people in the economic future of their own countries and of Europe as a whole."

On the contrary, commentators were alarmed by the "instability" of the American economy. Return to isolation, to protectionism, to all the other manifestations of economic nationalism which fear could conjure up was freely predicted. The deliberate judgment of the American people, therefore, that we could not live as an island of prosperity in a ruined world was a great decision. It was not made hastily or impulsively; definitive proof of this fact is furnished by the continuance of the Marshall appropriations to their appointed conclusion, and renewed assistance in other forms, but contributing to the same ends, ever since. No "five year plan" or any other economic program of nations neither democratic nor troubled by the lack of a strong executive was ever carried out more faithfully or more successfully.

The second fact is just as important: the decision to tax

ourselves to help Europe was not alone a decision of economic self-interest; it was a moral decision of the highest order of importance. One of the most experienced and articulate critics of our democratic foreign policy feels that the intrusion of moral principles distorts political judgment: "I see the most serious fault of our past policy formulation to lie in something that I might call the legalistic-moralistic approach to international problems." He would found policy upon a "careful appraisal of power factors" in the world; in effect, he accepts power politics as the central reality. Another writer, who equally dislikes moral considerations, would make geopolitics the touchstone of reality. Still another would draw a balance sheet of our resources and commitments, neglecting the greatest asset of all—the human spirit.

It is striking, therefore, that the most decisively successful piece of diplomacy since the war—the Marshall Plan—was based neither on power politics nor geopolitics nor economics alone; one of its chief characteristics was a profound moral commitment. Public acceptance of the Marshall Plan depended upon the conviction that the virtues of freedom are supreme, that freedom is indivisible, and that we bear a heavy responsibility not only for its survival but also for its spread to the rest of the world.

In this great gesture there was something of the moral grandeur of Lincoln's Second Inaugural. That address came from a man who had purged his soul of rancor and bitterness, and sought healing and recovery. The younger Charles Francis Adams wrote to his father, our minister in London, that Lincoln "has shown a capacity for rising to the demands of the hour which we should not expect from orators or men of the schools. This inaugural strikes me in its grand simplicity and directness as being for all time the historical keynote of the war; in it a people seemed to speak in the sublimely simple utterance of ruder times."

The Marshall Plan had a like moral elevation, a breadth of outlook which distinguishes statesmanship from the maneuvers of petty politicians. It has well been said that it earned for the United States the moral leadership of the world. The fact that it has paid rich rewards politically in stabilizing Western Europe and helping to cement the Atlantic alliance, and handsome dividends in trade and prosperity, does not withdraw one whit from its moral grandeur.

Again the Marshall Plan is no argument from the particular to the general. The first loan to Britain, the Truman Doctrine with its rescue of Greece and Turkey, the creation of UNRRA, NATO, and many other accomplishments could be cited to show that democracy can reach hard decisions. They supply evidence that many judgments will be right, that public opinion can form a reasonably accurate estimate of the situation and act responsibly to meet its demands.

10

Maturity

These statements involve no implicit claim that the United States is superior to other free nations. The Organization for European Economic Cooperation, the European Payments Union, the Coal-Steel Community, and many another European action and decision belie the inference that mass democracy is ill-disciplined and unwilling to sacrifice present comfort for future benefit. Stress has been laid on the United States because the effectiveness of its structure for policy making has been called into question so frequently and with such vigor and directness. There has been a great deal of talk, some abroad, but much more here at home, of our "immaturity" in foreign affairs.

It is true that we came late to the world scene, that, in this sense, we do not have so much experience as some nations. But there is much to be said on the other side which is just as important. One outstanding advantage of the United States is almost always forgotten because we have become so accustomed to it that it seems as natural as breathing. Our nation is composed of forty-eight sovereign states. They are tied together in the Federal Union. With customary extravagance it has been asserted that their authority has shrunk to impotence, their powers have withered away as the Federal government has taken over many functions and "monopolized" the taxing power. To some extent these things have happened; nonetheless the states still retain large areas of individual responsibility. More specifically, when they choose to do so, they can hurt each other by taxation, embargoes, quarantines, and dozens of other means.

This is done sometimes. The silver bloc has exacted a toll from the rest of the nation which constitutes a serious loss. Many other illustrations could be found. If all these harmful actions were added together and looked at by themselves, they would seem so impressive that a stranger might gain the notion that the Union was not very effective. When, however, these manifestations of negative separatism are compared with the evidences of regional and national co-operation between the states, they sink into relative insignificance. In short, we have learned domestically that the beggar-my-neighbor policy is self-defeating. In this experience there has been much that is valid for world affairs. We have been helped toward maturity of outlook in international matters because of the quasi-international character of our Union.

Some claim the United States is at a disadvantage because of the Constitutional separation of powers, which poses some difficulties in the management of foreign relations, though they are greatly exaggerated by the proponents of a strong executive. The tragedy of Woodrow Wilson is often cited as a dramatic illustration of presidential frustration by the Congress. Yet that is hardly an instance of inherent weakness in American government. Wilson had a genius for making his own path difficult. For example, he failed to treat international affairs in a broadly bipartisan or unpartisan spirit. The only Republican member of the Paris peace delegation was Henry White, an admirable man, well known as one of the earliest of our new body of professional diplomats. But he had no such political standing as to justify his appointment as a representative Republican; indeed, this designation looked like an evasion of the issue and was so regarded by party leaders. If Wilson was not adequately flexible or conciliatory, Senator Lodge, on the other side, typified in a singularly bitter and obstructive way the injection of partisanship into foreign affairs.

The lesson of that disastrous episode in our history is not so much the revelation of a weakness in the structure of our government as proof that the human equation is central to any system. In Britain the decline to impotence of the Liberal party, the difficulties of Attlee in dealing with Bevanism exhibited the same sort of thing. And French politics often seem to center in persons and their mutual animosities rather than issues. Nor is free government the only kind where personal traits affect large issues. The purges of the Soviet regime reveal the intensity of the struggle for personal power in nations with "strong leadership." The personal antagonisms that exist even under rigorous party discipline were exposed to the world by the statements of the new Soviet leaders at the Party Congress early in 1956.

Despite all difficulties, our experience in policy formation and action since the last war has been relatively satisfactory. The name of Arthur Vandenburg is symbolic. He had been an isolationist; in a speech of rare courage he announced his conversion; then in a post of great influence and substantial power he subordinated every other consideration to what he called "unpartisanship" in foreign affairs. In the Eighty-fourth Congress Senator George has displayed the same elevated spirit. It cannot be said that politics stops at the low-tide shoreline, but at that point it does take on a bland quality that is missing on many domestic issues.

In any event, we should not decry all political disagreement in foreign affairs. There are very few policies that are completely black or totally white; there are even fewer implementations of policy that are perfectly adapted to their purposes. The complexities of international affairs are so many and so intricate that consistency in meeting all of them is rare indeed. The plain fact is that debate—even partisan debate—helps to mold decision and action through enlightenment as well as compromise. Purists will say that compromise dilutes policy and makes it by so much ineffective for its purpose. The point can be conceded without serious loss. Crystal-clear policy might be made in a political vacuum; but human nature abhors that condition and will not let it continue. Even in a totalitarian nation the bureaucracy would not tolerate it; and in a democracy the crystal-clear policy would fail because it would have no consensus of public opinion behind it. Under such circumstances it would fail at home, even though it might be momentarily effective abroad.

Some scholars, some commentators, some professional diplomats resent politics, either frankly or subconsciously. They prefer *expertise* of their own particular brand to the democratic hurly-burly by which issues are shaped (even if they are not defined or clarified) and enough agreement reached to permit some action, wise or unwise—effective, useless, or vicious. They may as well remember, however, that it is either democracy and the democratic way, or something a lot worse—a dictator's whim, palace intrigue, a bureaucracy, a military clique, an economic pressure group, or some other dominant force.

This reinforces the point made earlier that diplomacy moves in the medium of politics; there is no other atmosphere available, and it is folly to seek one. Schemes for the elimination of political forces in diplomacy are simply efforts to evade the facts of life. It is absurd to find men arguing for such a utopian program while pretending to deal realistically with world problems.

It is again a reminder, and a necessary one, that the professional should never be supreme. The ordinary man who wants a home could not draw the designs, write the specifications, and supervise the construction. Nevertheless, he should have the last word in dealing with the professionals who are, after all, working for him. If it is possible, they should see that he gets what he wants. In the educational world presidents and provosts, who, some of us are convinced, are men of infinite wisdom, are nonetheless subject to boards of trustees, to their occasional great discomfort—and benefit. It is a vital part of our Constitutional system that the professional soldier should always be subject to civilian direction; that provision was not made through inadvertence but was founded upon hard experience. It is especially true that in diplomacy the professional should never have the last word.

These things being so, if we want improvement in the realm of international relations, we are cast back upon public education, as was pointed out earlier. Of course I mean education in the broadest sense. There is no hope of throwing the whole burden of developing public competence in foreign affairs upon the schools at any particular level, or at all levels added together. There is no compact body of knowledge, no well-defined discipline which can be guaranteed to produce an informed, alert, wise, and morally sensitive citizenry. History, the literatures, philosophy, economics —in short, the liberal arts—are the media through which formal education must work. But anyone beyond his raw novitiate knows that the same body of facts, the same facility in rational processes will bring every variety of response from students. The sooner we face this truth and rely upon indirect means to teach citizenship and other public virtues, the faster we shall progress.

Certainly the schools are vital; but they are the smallest part of the educational process of which I speak. What a student may learn by facing citizenlike problems, if they can be related to his schooling, is significant. However, most public problems, fortunately, are not only remote, they are quite unreal to children; adults meet them in wholly different dimensions. People who are through with formal schooling read the newspapers, hear and read the commentators, see television and movie news. In traveling about the country, I buy newspapers in many cities; the astonishing fact today, as compared with a quarter of a century ago, is not the dearth of international news but its plentiful character.

People discuss in many different social and business circles what they hear and read and what they think. It was said over a century ago that when two Americans were talking together on a public question both seemed to be making a speech. In de Tocqueville's phrase, "an American cannot converse—he speaks to you as if he were addressing a meeting." Thus private conversations took on many of the elements of a town meeting.

There is an important book yet to be written on the invisible government of the United States. It is not the sinister force that the phrase "invisible government" suggests to many minds. On the contrary, the invisible element consists of the infinite number of voluntary organizations which distinguish our way of life. Americans have a positive genius for joining; where two or three are gathered together, there a bylaw appears. If all the bylaws of all our organizations were added together and compared with the total for the rest of the world, they would make our dominance in the number of telephones and motor cars seem trivial.

When people do not actually join committees or societies, they sign papers. I do not know how many invitations have come to my desk in the last year to sign a letter to the President, or an open letter to the Press, for some cause. Usually, but not always, the objective was good; sometimes, though good it seemed unwise. Nevertheless, there was never a dearth of signers.

Voluntary association, based on the urge to "do something about it," appears in myriad forms both permanent and transient. Many such organizations have been classed as pressure groups, and the phrase has often been used in a derogatory sense. Such general denunciation is quite wrong. Our Constitution set up the government of the United States as a complex piece of machinery, but it provided no source of energy to run it. One of the chief evidences that our Founders were not all-wise was their attitude toward parties; they regarded them as "factions," and unworthy. Even before Washington's administration closed it became evident (though not to all contemporaries) that parties must supply the drive to operate the machinery of our government.

That has been the historic function of parties. Sometimes, and on some issues, they have some ideological characteristics. But the Democratic party is essentially liberal in the North, conservative in the South. In states where the Republicans are so dominant as not to be seriously challenged it is not uncommon to find one Senator a liberal and the other a conservative. In short, the national parties are combinations of local entities which themselves lack not only ideological consistency but any coherent ideological content.

This is bound to be true because party discipline is so lax that political heresy, if it could be established, could not be punished. In Britain unless a man has a peculiarly solid hold upon his own constituency—as has Aneurin Bevan, for example—the discipline available to party managers is very severe; indeed many believe it has gone too far in exercising control over individual members. In this country even Franklin Roosevelt with his vast popularity could not "purge" dissident members of his party from office. A Representative, living in his Congressional district, can gain so firm a hold upon the electorate as to defy every effort to subject him to party pressure. A Senator with his six-year term of office is still more immune.

These circumstances open the way for pressure groups to function. There are many, many channels through which they can exercise political influence. Even more important, they carry on political education. When an individual joins others to "do something about it," he usually wants to know what he is doing something about, and why. That is the perfect setting for self-education, motivation at its best. Many efforts have been made to formalize and systematize that process through reading clubs, discussion groups, and the like. It is in no sense an underestimation of their value to assert that the voluntarism of spontaneous pressure groups should not be discounted either.

From a scholar's point of view, or from the angle of vision of a time-weary columnist, or from the observation of a professional diplomat, these methods of education may seem not only inadequate but pitifully so. On the contrary, they are sufficient so long as public opinion is not expected to deal in nuances, in procedures, in techniques. Actually it needs only to respond to situations in clear and simple terms. For example, public opinion must decide that the United States is to go it alone or have a "career in the world"; it must determine to let the devil take the hindmost or temper competition with cooperation; it must agree or refuse to pay the bill for deterrent armaments; it must weary of the stridency of the chauvinist, the exploiter of issues—and show its disapproval; it must cut down to size the politician grown "too big for his britches"; it must bring the moral simplicity of the golden rule to bear upon international issues.

11

The Alternatives

Earlier, when discussing the Marshall Plan, I noted the tendency of modern critics to ignore—even to deplore—the spiritual, moral, and religious elements so characteristic of, and so essential to, democracy. It is worth re-emphasizing how astounding it is to find one of our most literate critics, in the light of America's achievements over the years, suggest that our methods of policy making should be altered and henceforth be calculated upon the basis of a balance sheet of commitments and assets. It is equally amazing that another critic, also much in the public eye, decries the tendency to inject morality into policy which, he feels, should be founded upon cold calculations of power.

Consider what the consequences of such programs would have been in well-remembered historical situations. For example, what policy would the balance sheet principle have suggested for Britain after the Low Countries had been overrun and France had collapsed? Would it not have been surrender on the best terms available? On any accounting of tangible assets and liabilities the policy of stubborn resistance, "on the beaches," "on the landing grounds," "in the fields and in the streets," was bankrupt.

If, following the pattern proposed by another critic, the course of action were controlled by a "careful appraisal of power factors," would not that procedure also have revealed the hopelessness of such dogged resistance? Yet the battle of Britain was won; that is historic fact. The weakness of both critical proposals is the same: they fail to take into account the human spirit.

That spirit was typified by the indomitable will of a pudgy figure forever making a V sign with his fingers, who could take common English words, frame them into simple sentences, utter them in a hesitant manner in a voice that lacked resonance, yet could stiffen the spine of Caspar Milquetoast and make "the timid soul" into "something of a hero." The Battle of Britain was won by heart, by courage, by faith—far more significant in sound policy making than all the detached calculations proposed by pessimists regarding democracy.

Or look at India. By what balance-sheet technique could Gandhi have been encouraged to strive for the independence of that subcontinent? What "appraisal of power factors" could have led him to hope for success? None, none whatever. He relied upon "soul force" which the doubting realists never mention because it is something they cannot understand. The drive for independence did not center in any great intellectual concept; some of Gandhi's economic ideas seem incredibly naïve. Nevertheless, his homespun, hand-woven cloth and his austere diet of goats' milk supplied the complete and final answer to economic determinists with their crass materialism. He refuted for all time the soundness of the argument for exclusive dependence upon power politics.

On any of these proposed bases of policy calculation how could one account for a man who exercised at least as much influence from a jail cell as when he was at large? It did no good to shut Gandhi up. Nor did the rulers of a vast empire dare to let him die of self-imposed fasting despite the fact that he lived in a country where literally hundreds of thousands have no homes, where unnumbered thousands die from malnutrition and lack of sanitation, without any medical care whatever. This would indicate that life is held cheap; yet so potent would Gandhi's voluntary martyrdom have been that none could face the consequences. His spirit so moved masses of men that they followed after him as a prophet; they revered him as a saint. Ultimately "soul force" defeated every other kind of power, and India attained independence without war. To overlook the significance of so massive an event in considering how to frame policy is to "pay tithe of mint and anise and cummin, and have omitted the weightier matters of the law, judgment, mercy, and faith."

Or consider the whole nationalist movement in Southeast Asia, North Africa, and elsewhere. It cannot be explained, much less justified, on any power estimates or balance-sheet technique. It arises from the yearning of men to be themselves, even at the cost of comfort or life itself, rather than remain as well-kept wards. From most material points of view colonial peoples would be "better off" to come to their freedom more gradually. But they weary, as men should, of tutelage, however benevolent. Charles Malik, who represented Lebanon at the United Nations for some years, expressed the thought with great force: "Europe has taught the world that no greater disgrace can befall one people than to be politically subject to another. This lesson Asia has learned with a vengeance."

We need not appeal only to foreign experience. American policy likewise demonstrates the validity of intangibles. When he was Secretary of State, Mr. Acheson rightly spoke of the desirability of negotiating from "situations of strength." We have built that strength, through NATO, and other alliances, and by our own efforts. It is indubitable that our leadership in the atomic race, our far-flung bases, and all the panoply of our power gave the Soviets pause. At the same time it strongly tended to awe the neutrals, and raised questions in their minds regarding our ultimate intentions. The uncommitted peoples worried lest we be tempted by our very power to employ it in a "preventive war." So long as we spoke chiefly of capacity for massive retaliation at times and places of our own choosing that fear did not abate; it grew.

President Eisenhower brought a new emphasis into discussions. He spoke of spiritual strength as primary, as more important than economic strength or military might. Jaded journalists jeered at his "little homilies." Let us concede that there were no winged words or witty epigrams in what he said. Nonetheless the new emphasis evoked a response in the hearts of men and women. Then, at Geneva, with the spotlight of world attention focused directly upon him, he laid aside his glasses and the carefully drafted text and spoke directly and simply from the heart. Even the Russians believed him. Integrity beyond challenge, faith in the reality and vitality of spiritual forces—these things produced a better effect upon doubting nations than a show of force could ever achieve.

To what conclusion do we come? Situations of strength are still essential; a reasonable estimate of the relationship of commitments to potentialities is ordinary prudence. But armaments, economic strength, alliances are not enough. Policy must also be based upon moral considerations as well as the more tangible factors. The human spirit cannot be entered upon a balance sheet, nor weighed, nor measured, nor counted. Yet it remains the most potent force in all the world. Plain people know this instinctively; they respond to its manifestations wherever they appear throughout the globe.

Democracy itself finds its root in the equality of men, which is explicable upon no basis except religious grounds. Public opinion provides the strongest foundation for diplomacy when spiritual strength is given its rightful position of priority among all the factors that shape policy.

Set in Linotype No. 21
Format by Stephen King
Manufactured by The Haddon Craftsmen, Inc.
Published by HARPER & BROTHERS, *New York*